Illustrated
ASTON
MARTIN
BUYER'S
GUIDE™

Illustrated
ASTON MARTIN
BUYER'S GUIDE ™·

Paul R. Woudenberg

Motorbooks International
Publishers & Wholesalers Inc
Osceola, Wisconsin 54020, USA ®

First published in 1986 by Motorbooks
International Publishers & Wholesalers Inc,
PO Box 2, 729 Prospect Avenue, Osceola,
WI 54020 USA

Library of Congress Cataloging-in-Publication Data

Woudenberg, Paul R.
    Illustrated Aston Martin buyer's guide.

    1. Aston Martin automobile.   2. Automobiles—
Purchasing.   I. Title.
TL215.A75W68   1986   629.2'222   85-25935
ISBN 0-87938-210-4 (pbk.)

Printed and bound in the United States of
America

Cover photograph: 1962 Aston Martin DB4GT
Zagato by Roger Stowers

Sole distribution in the United Kingdom by
Motor Racing Publications Limited,
Unit 6,
The Pilton Estate,
46 Pitlake,
CROYDON, CR0 3RY, England

Foreword

The first thing that struck me when I began this foreword for Paul Woudenberg's wonderful book on Aston Martin, was that more than thirty-five years have passed since my personal introduction to the marque.

Since then, the company has been through various ups and downs and a reorganization or two, but the one thing that has remained is the basic philosophy toward making automobiles—always of the highest order. In driving an Aston of today and one of thirty-five years ago, one senses immediately the lineage.

I have owned many cars over the years and my DB2, bought new in 1951, ranks, along with a few others, right at the top in owner satisfaction. The Aston had so few annoyances and so many pleasurable aspects that I still think of it today as a measure of what the joys of car ownership can be.

My experience with Aston Martin has continued partly through my long acquaintance with John Wyer and by my having driven on the works team at Le Mans in 1963. More recently, I have had the thrill of lapping at over 170 mph at Wolfsburg, Germany, in one of the current coupes—an outstanding example of a luxury GT car that has been around awhile, and continues to hold its own.

If there is one element in Aston Martin's existence that I can especially relate to, it is the racing record. From the first time I saw the Aston Martins at Le Mans in 1952, where five cars started and all cars finished, I was impressed and proud, since I was an Aston owner at the time. Throughout those years, wherever they were entered, the Astons were highly competitive and greatly respected. I remember well our Ferrari team being soundly beaten by Stirling Moss in an Aston in the late fifties at the Nürburgring 1,000 km race. It was always amazing to me to watch the extraordinary road holding exhibited by the Astons at the "Ring." After Stirling took the lead from me in 1958 I was able to stay behind him for a short while and watch the behavior of the car. It was a wonderful sight to see.

All in all, the most remarkable thing is that in times such as these the company has been able to remain in existence. It speaks highly for the total Aston Martin following, both past and present. The Aston Martin Owners Club is very strong and certainly deserves much credit in helping to keep the company alive and well. Dr. Woudenberg's fine work is long overdue and should be most welcome to all Aston enthusiasts.

Phil Hill

Contents

Acknowledgments

The Aston Martin fraternity is helpful and encouraging and I wish to thank so many who have given freely of their time. Ken Boyd, of Aston Martin Services, shared a lifetime of experience in reading the manuscript and his associate, Walt Powell, made numerous important contributions. Doug Ritter of Tucson, formerly the parts and purchasing manager with the US distributors in King of Prussia, PA, and later in New Rochelle, NY, made a painstaking analysis with major suggestions. Derrick Edwards, the world authority on prewar cars of Morntane Engineering in London, generously opened his picture archives and also read the prewar material.

Roger Stowers, in Newport Pagnell, England, contributed many hours in sharing his intimate knowledge of the cars and the company and gave the manuscript a close scrutiny with much useful advice. He also was exceptionally generous in providing a great number of superb pictures. Michael Bowler, a gifted writer and the multitalented chief engineer at Aston Martin Lagonda, was very helpful.

I am grateful to Phil Hill for his trenchant suggestions and his eloquent preface. Barbara Harold, as usual, is a superb editor who saves so many from folly. Tim Parker was particularly helpful in providing needed contacts in England and in shaping the book.

Many owners and enthusiasts have graciously contributed pictures. Aston Publications has generously provided rare photos from Dr. T. C. March. Others who have been helpful are Dudley Heath, Richard Habershon and P.H.U. Blume in England, Jerry Rosenstock, George Sidman, Ted Reich, Gary D. Moore and Dean Batchelor in the US, and Robert Follows in Vancouver.

A basic source for all writers on Aston Martin is *The Aston Martin Register*, published by the club. The compilers of the Register, Jane Archer, Tony Byles, Inman Hunter and Alan Archer, have done an extraordinary job in assembling specification and history on the cars and the company. I want to acknowledge, with deep gratitude, my indebtedness to their work and commend the Register to all prospective buyers.

Last but hardly least, I am deeply indebted to that ebullient genius who guides the fortunes of the company, Victor Gauntlett, whose business acumen is matched by his love and deep knowledge of the cars.

It is always the goal of an author to produce a perfect or, at the least, an error-free book. Perfection is not granted in this life and any remaining errors are mine. Criticisms and suggestions from readers are very welcome.

Paul R. Woudenberg, PhD
Pebble Beach, May 1986

Introduction

The buyer of an Aston Martin automobile joins one of the most distinguished automotive fraternities in the world. Such a claim rests upon several observations.

1. The Aston Martin has origins dating from 1914 and production dating from 1921, a record for specialist automobile producers. A principal rival of the Aston Martin, the Ferrari, dates only from 1948, while Maserati production, though beginning in 1926, consisted only of competition cars until after World War II.

2. Few companies have had such a long, independent life as Aston Martin. The firm has had its crises but has managed to recover each time with renewed vigor. Only the Morgan, beginning in 1910, has had a longer life as a small, independent specialist firm, but even then its four-wheel automobile production was not begun until 1936.

3. No company has been able to maintain such a consistent focus as Aston Martin. As founded by Lionel Martin and Robert Bamford in 1913, the company has devoted itself to the highest-quality sports and touring cars with a focus on racing. With each reconstitution as a company, the founding goal was reaffirmed and enhanced. Even the great Bentley suffered a substantial change of image in 1933 and again in 1946 which eventually led to a car indistinguishable from the Rolls-Royce.

4. By virtue of this long production life and consistent focus, the Aston Martin automobile remains a fascinating prospect, no matter what vintage one may choose to buy. The prewar cars are beautifully made with elegant low lines. The postwar cars through the DB2/4 Mark III retain a very strong identifying look and a unique mechanical description, essentially "sporting" in feel. The later-production cars beginning with the DB4 are splendid grand touring machines able to challenge any rivals. From time to time exotic racing cars may be found. An Aston Martin of any type and time is a thoroughbred.

5. The buyer of an Aston Martin benefits from a substantial body of literature. Some of the best automotive writers have been drawn to the marque and the general quality of writing and production values is far above the average. This is the sign of a great motorcar. It may be truthfully said that there is no bad book on Aston Martins and there are many fine ones. The quality of the car seems to elicit a high level of research and effort.

6. The Aston Martin is further helped by an excellent group of enthusiasts who comprise the Aston Martin Owners Club (AMOC). This is the oldest club devoted to a sporting vehicle and began in May 1935,

exactly a year before the rival Bentley Driver's Club. The first president of the AMOC was the renowned Charles Jarrott, a great pioneer in motor racing. He was succeeded by no less than S.C.H. "Sammy" Davis, whose combined excellence as a driver and writer has never been exceeded. Early leadership of this stature quickly established the AMOC in the forefront of enthusiast motoring, a tradition which has continued to this day.

7. A strong club is more than a great history. The AMOC has a fine publications program which is extremely valuable to its widespread membership. The *Aston Martin Magazine* is a high-quality quarterly with color covers. The *Aston Martin News Sheet* appears monthly. There are also regional news bulletins which enhance the strong sense of "connection" for owners of Aston Martins.

8. The club produces a register from time to time (currently 268 pages), which is quite likely the finest of its type in the world. Every car in the club is listed with relevant racing, rallying and concours history. (Since 1977, only the best three results per car per year are listed.) In addition, an exceptionally useful technical description is given of each model—an invaluable resource when identifying cars. Production figures and dates are included. In short, the register is a basic research tool and is a tribute to the skills and tremendous efforts of club members. In particular, appreciation should be given for the devoted services of the editors: Jane Archer, Tony Byles, Inman Hunter and Alan Archer.

9. The club also produces a membership list (eighty pages), again beautifully produced and organized—no computer printouts from the AMOC!

10. Owners of Aston Martins have long taken comfort in the ready availability of most parts. The factory offers excellent service for all models beginning with the DB6. Ivan Forshaw's Aston Service Dorset, Ltd. (73 Ringwood Road, Longham, Wim-borne, Dorset) is the official agent for spares for the DB2 through the DB5. Morntane Engineering (College Yard, Highgate, London, NW5 1NX) caters to prewar cars. Aston Martin Services (2381 American Avenue, Hayward, California, 94545), an agent for the Dorset company, provides US owners with postwar items. Aston Martin owners have not been "orphaned" and the survival rate of the cars is high.

11. All of this support contributes to the marketability of the car. The value of the Aston Martin remains consistent. This is caused, in addition, by the rapid rise in price of the new car in the seventies, which has tended to draw used-car values upward. The Aston Martin today is a very expensive automobile, and this has helped the image of the older cars.

12. The high current price has further helped the older-car market because it has encouraged investment in restoration. This is important because of the substantial number of Aston Martins available in the postwar market. There were 1,782 normal-production cars produced at Feltham from 1948 to 1959, according to the register. Beginning with the DB4 in 1958 there have been over 7,500 cars built at Newport Pagnell. Buyers have a broad choice.

13. Membership in the Aston Martin Owners Club offers yet another advantage. There are still inexpensive Aston Martins available but they usually require major restoration. These cars attract enthusiasts. A low first price may encourage buyers of modest means to enter the market with the intent of home restoration and with the long-range hope of a fair return upon sale. Such cars, restored by talented amateurs (and usually club members), may be the best buys of all since such labor is, all too often, impossible to recover in a sale price. A car bought from an enthusiast club member may be a superior investment.

Thus, the Aston Martin combines myriad sound reasons for luring potential buyers. But perhaps the greatest reasons lie in those indefinable subjective matters which are at the heart of all collecting. The Aston Martin, of whatever vintage, is a pleasure to drive and always a thoroughbred. It is a car that rewards skill. Some models are blindingly fast; all are beautifully made. The owner of an Aston Martin may be proud of such a car whose cachet of excellence and good breeding remains obvious to all.

Pricing

Estimated prices are quoted in either sterling (£) or US dollars ($). There are several reasons for not converting all prices to one currency.

1. The exchange rate varies. In 1984 the swing between sterling and dollars was substantial. Prices did not move with like speed. Conversion at any fixed rate is thus misleading.

2. Aston Martin owners in the US are usually very knowledgeable about the UK market and have little trouble dealing with currency rates. Such knowledge will play an important part in deciding where to shop.

3. The prices quoted reflect the source of information, whether in the UK or the US.

Investment rating

Investment rating system

A five-star system pioneered by Dean Batchelor for this buyer's guide series and used by the author in a previous work is here continued with appropriate modifications.

★ A model which has not drawn the attention or enthusiasm of collectors. Usually readily available. May have good potential.

★★ A model which has found excitement and support from enthusiasts and which is well worth substantial restoration investment.

★★★ A model of particular collectibility which has shown strong price advance in recent years and which is now much sought after. Older cars may be hard to find.

★★★★ A rare model of great desirability with assured future value.

★★★★★ A car of exceptional interest, rarity and value.

Some further notes on ratings:

1. Open-bodied versions of models that usually have closed coachwork will bring fifty percent to one hundred percent premiums and receive a one-star upgrade.

2. Prices are greatly dependent on condition, and no guide can make up for the experienced eye of an appraiser. The prices quoted in this book are for premium-condition cars unless otherwise stated. Restoration costs can be very high and should be deducted from estimated values.

3. Opinions on prices have been sought from all quarters by the author. Sources include recognized experts in the field, owners, dealers and information from verified recent sales and auctions.

4. Often peak prices are long remembered even when the market may not follow. The price may not represent the market. Such peak prices are noted in the text.

5. Buying and selling used cars is done in a wonderful and virtually unique open marketplace. Intelligence, patience and study are greatly rewarded.

This buyer's guide is dedicated to helping Aston Martin buyers find a good car at a fair price. Fortunately, the Aston Martin fraternity is filled with fine and honest enthusiasts whose appreciation of the car is one of the best reasons for confidence by the buyer. Aston Martin owners jealously guard the reputation and integrity of this superb automobile.

Chapter 1

The Lionel Martin cars ★★

★★★Twin Cam

```
1914-1925
Production: 63 cars total
(eight are listed in the current register and
twelve others may still exist)
        production cars              50
        prototypes and specials      13
```

History

Before World War I, Lionel Martin tuned and raced a Singer 10 which he had bought in 1912. In 1913, he formed a limited company with Robert Bamford in South Kensington, London. Using a 1389 cc Coventry-Climax engine and a 1908 Isotta-Fraschini chassis, a hybrid car was constructed which is considered the first Aston Martin. Another car, the Coal Scuttle was built in 1915.

In 1922, Bamford sold his interst in the company to Martin, who then proceeded to build several prototypes and racing cars, the most successful of which was powered by a new side-valve engine of 1486 cc. There were numerous exotic-engined specials with single and double overhead cams and several single-seat racing cars. The first sale of production cars began in 1923.

In July 1924 the company was refinanced when Lady Charnwood bought the assets on behalf of her son, John Benson. But this new promise was short-lived. Though the firm exhibited at the Olympia show in October 1925, production had ceased and a receiver was appointed on November 11. On November 13, Lionel Martin left the firm. (This early history is exceptionally interesting, especially the racing successes. The reader is referred to Inman Hunter's *Aston Martin 1914 to 1940: A Pictorial Review.* Hunter is also responsible, with F. E. Ellis, for book one (1921-1940) of *Aston Martin, The Story of a Sports Car,* compiled by Dudley Coram, in which a much-expanded version is presented. See also A. B. Demaus' *Lionel Martin, A Biography,* and Geoff Courtney's *The Power behind Aston Martin.*)

Identification

Serial numbers for the earliest period begin at 1910 and conclude with 1969. Perhaps twenty of these cars survive in the hands of dedicated enthusiasts, so any buyer may expect detailed history.

Performance and utility

The 1486 cc engine produced 38 bhp at 5.5:1 compression and 45 bhp at 5.8:1—remarkable for the time. Back axle ratio was 3.73, numerically low for such a small engine which permitted high cruising speeds. Despite the sporting background, buyers often opted for the long chassis of 105 inches over the short chassis of ninety-six inches. Top speed was about 70 mph but useful cruising speed was more like 50 mph.

The 16 valve twin-cam engine (this one is number 1961) developed 55 bhp at 4200 rpm in its initial form. It was a sophisticated engine which was based on the Ernest Henri three-liter GP Ballot design. Only a handful of these engines were built. Derrick Edwards archives

Perhaps six of the twin-cam sixteen-valve racing cars have survived; these had 55 bhp and a top speed of 90 mph. These engines are currently being developed to produce as much as 80 bhp.

Problem areas

Collectors of these very early cars have familiarity with the need for the "in house" production of spares, as none are presently stocked by any supplier. Fortunately, these first Aston Martins were well made and established the reputation of the marque. Reliability may be expected under moderate use. If prepared correctly, a twin-cam model can be reliable even under racing conditions.

Coachwork

Early Aston Martins had numerous body switches prior to serious production in

This 1925 16 valve twin-cam team car, number 1961, has an illustrious competition history. It was rebuilt by both Lord Charnwood and Derrick Edwards and has continued to be raced to the present time. Rare or unique examples of these early cars bring high prices. Derrick Edwards archives

The oldest "active" Aston Martin is this 1922 car named Green Pea, which has had a complicated history involving engines, registration and chassis number swaps. In its original form it appeared at Strasbourg at the French Grand Prix in 1922 and was driven by Zborowski. It is here driven by Morris Goodall, a former works driver and founding member of the Aston Martin Owners Club. Owner Neil Murray looks on. Roger Stowers photo

Green Pea at speed at a Horsfall meeting. The balance of the design is evident. This rare car with a fine racing history commands a very high price. Roger Stowers photo

1923. After 1923, the proclivity of owners to compete with their cars often resulted in specials with exiguous coachwork. Aston Martin enthusiasts would be delighted to own one of these rare early models regardless of coachwork, but body originality remains the best goal.

Summary and prospects

The rarity of the pre-1925 Lionel Martin cars makes any market estimates difficult. Not only is the market very small, but the early cars are not in great demand because they are slow and noncompetitive. Nevertheless, pride of ownership is very high and the willingness of owners to part with such rare specimens remains the key factor. Those interested in speculation should not apply. Proven enthusiasm, long club membership and patience make up the best path toward ownership.

A fine restored side-valve car may now be worth about £25,000. A 1923 GP was recently on offer at £40,000. Ordinary examples will be much less expensive.

A 1925 GP car, number 1934, which was raced by George Eyston. This car was fitted with a side valve engine but was soon replaced with a 16 valve unit. Roger Stowers photo

Chapter 2

1½ liter, first series; tourer, sports, International and Le Mans

★★★

1927-January 1932
Production: 129 cars total
(perhaps eighty survive)

History

The name of Aston Martin was already of such excellence that the firm was not allowed to die. The rescuer was Augustus C. Bertelli, a brilliant engineer and driver whose talents had produced a sporting version of the Enfield-Allday in 1922. With William Somerville Renwick, Bertelli had formed an engine-manufacturing company in 1924 whose first product was a 1495 cc sohc engine which was fitted into an Enfield-Allday chassis. The two refounded Aston Martin in October 1926, joining the Charnwood family which had purchased the assets of Bamford and Martin for £10,000. Important to the project was a new leased factory at Feltham. Various investors appeared, but the company was usually in near-crisis conditions.

The first-series car was entirely new. The engine was the Renwick and Bertelli sohc unit of 1495 cc which produced 56 bhp at 4250 rpm. A separate gearbox and a worm-geared back axle completed the drivetrain. The large, fourteen-inch brakes were unusual in a light car.

A very few cars (about fifteen) were built initially on a conventional chassis with a 120 inch wheelbase. A sporting model was soon available on a short 102 inch chassis which featured the axle over the frame and which would become the standard layout. This first International series formed the backbone of early production and was usually fitted with a 2/4 seat touring body. The wet-sump engine of the initial touring cars was modified to a dry-sump unit for the International and a long-chassis version replaced the initial touring series.

Two factory team cars, three seaters, were raced at Le Mans in 1928 and LM1 was the first Aston Martin to have the familiar enameled badge. A cataloged Le Mans model was offered in 1931 and six were built in the first series. An uprated engine called the Ulster (the first use of that term) was available for £50 extra.

Identification

The first-series 1½ established the Aston Martin "look," in particular the cycle fenders closely mounted on the brake backing plates of the twenty-one-inch wheels. The under-slung chassis gave the cars a very low look. The separate gearbox and worm-drive back axle identified the first series.

Chassis numbers: 1001, 1002, then 3 to A2/129. Various prefixes were used. In the early numbers up to 73, T=long chassis,

This standard International was built in 1930. The 1495 cc engine produced 56 bhp. When tested by *The Autocar* in 1931, this model achieved 75 mph. Fine examples may now bring around £20,000. Derrick Edwards archives

This one-off coupe body on this 1930 International sets it apart from the usual tourers. It is particularly handsome. The engine was bored out to two liters in the early thirties and reputedly had a speed near 100 mph. Derrick Edwards archives

S=short chassis. A new system was then introduced in which the first letter (A through L) indicates the month, and the following number indicates year (for example, 0=1930). Also, LM signifies factory team cars. (Consult the Aston Martin Register to verify any car.)

Performance and utility

The wonderful close-ratio box, always an Aston Martin strong point, coupled with a robust and willing engine made these cars a delight to drive. But they were heavy. An ordinary 1930 International owned by Dudley Coram was reported by him to weigh 19 cwt (2,128 lb). Maximum speed was quoted by numerous contemporary testers in the region of 80 mph. But the car was truly strained at these speeds and Coram suggested speeds in the low seventies as more realistic. In today's usage, prudent cruising speeds are much lower. Acceleration is modest.

Thanks to the resources of Morntane Engineering in Highgate, spares for these and all prewar Aston Martins are available. Using today's available parts, engine revs can be safely sustained at 3500 rpm giving 68-70 mph with enough in hand for short bursts to 90 mph.

This 1930 International 2/4 seater, S40, is a handsome example of the first-series 1½ liter. The twin spares on the back are not usual but could have been useful in trials work by offering an alternate set of rear tires plus added rear weight. The worm drive axle, when properly set up and maintained, is usually trouble free. Richard Habershon photo

Problem areas

The weakness of the first series is the worm back axle, about which Bertelli himself confessed, "I never did make a decent rear axle," as Inman Hunter reports. In order to work on the back axle, the body usually must be removed! However, if rebuilt correctly the rear axle should prove reliable, especially under moderate usage. If clearances are checked, say every five years, no trouble should be encountered.

The engine is reliable but not easy to work on. Timing is difficult. All other parts of the car are immensely strong.

Coachwork

Harry Bertelli, Augustus Bertelli's brother, designed the bodies for the new cars, and they were universally handsome. The very

This fine example, number T14, of the ten-foot long-chassis tourer had unusually low lines for the time. Top speed approached 70 mph but with a 4.75:1 axle ratio the 1488 cc engine was asked for high revs. These long-chassis cars are rare, since enthusiasts have usually opted for the more sporting versions. Prices should be near those of the short-chassis models. Roger Stowers photo

low chassis presented design opportunities which were exploited. The Bertellis soon established the coachbuilding side as a separate company. Bertelli bodies are sturdy and somewhat heavy but seem to be long lasting.

There were also a few bodies mounted by outside firms including Barker, James Young, Harrison and Freestone & Webb, but none seem to have survived.

Summary and prospects

In this rarified market, prospective buyers are generally drawn from within the Aston Martin club. Owners are often reluctant to sell. The worm-drive cars are usually not quite as desirable as the later series but, nevertheless, prices can be high. Rough but complete examples may be £10,000, reasonable runners are priced at £15,000, and fine examples start around £20,000. Only two examples of the first-series Le Mans model survive.

The first team car, LM 1, was prepared in 1928 for Le Mans and was driven by Bertelli and Eyston and then sold to S.C.H. Davis in 1929. The filler for the dry-sump reservoir was directly in front of the radiator. Even with a weight of nearly 2,300 pounds the car was capable of 81 mph. Robert Follows photo

The first team car, LM 1, received steady development in the thirties under the ownership of S.C.H. Davis, who drove it perhaps 100,000 miles. The 21 inch wheels were replaced by 18 inch wheels in March 1936. LM 1 was further modified by the addition of a very large fuel tank, the rear mounting of the spare wheel and the squaring off of the rear body. Davis maintained that the car cruised best at 70 mph. The car has been restored by Robert Follows of Vancouver. Competition cars with full history and famous prior ownership are at the top of the market. Robert Follows photo

Chapter 3

1½ liter, second series   ★★★

February 1932-December 1933
Production: 130 cars total

History

The company went through another of its periodic crises and was refinanced by Sir Lancelot Prideaux Brune and a bit later by Arthur Sutherland. The car was redesigned with a Laycock gearbox attached to the engine and an ENV spiral-bevel differential. Prices were cut substantially.

The Le Mans model, as a true production job, appeared in October 1932 and soon replaced the New International. It was offered in both 2 and 2/4 seater coachwork. Le Mans engines had a 7.5:1 compression ratio (6.5:1 normal), and produced 70 bhp. The Le Mans gearbox had closer ratios.

A long-chassis (120 inches) standard model was offered (the 12/50) for tourer and saloon coachwork with a high radiator.

Identification

The second series had a slightly vee'd radiator, a unit engine and transmission, and bevel drive. The Le Mans models had slab-sided exposed fuel tanks and two raised cowlings over the instrument board (with two exceptions). Twin exhausts on the side were usual. The long-chassis models generally had swept fenders attached to the

body rather than the cycle fenders. Early production had twenty-one-inch wheels but eighteen-inch wheels soon were introduced.

Chassis numbers: B2/200 to L3/329/L. Letter=month, first number=year. (B2= February 1932, L3=December 1933.) LM= factory team cars.

Performance and utility

The New International four-seater, as tested by *Motor Sport* in 1932, returned a 0-60 mph time of about twenty-three seconds with a top of 70 mph. The dry-sump lubrication was one reason for the stamina of the engine at continued high revs. The Le Mans models were quicker, 0-60 taking twenty-two seconds, though *The Autocar* came up with just under twenty-five seconds. Top speed was 85 mph. The enemy was always weight, and even the Le Mans weighed at least 2,350 pounds. Handling was excellent.

Problem areas

With the new rear bevel axle, the principal weakness of the early cars was cured, and the second series has proven to be very durable.

Coachwork

Coachwork continued to be built by Bertelli. The long-chassis saloons and

This is an early 1932 Le Mans model, chassis G2/214, with the characteristic raised cowlings over the instrument panel. This car is not only very clean but has had an excellent competition history. The radiator blanking plate is happy evidence of cool running. Prices for good Le Mans models are well over £20,000. Derrick Edwards archives

A 1933 Le Mans model showing the very low chassis and tight mounting of the cycle fenders. It was expensive at £595 but the quality was evident. Derrick Edwards archives

tourers were poor sellers and Inman Hunter reports that only twenty were turned out.

This picture, taken in 1937, is of an International two-seater, D2/203, with a body from LM 8. In the driver's seat is a proud Richard Habershon, cigarette at a jaunty angle, the whole an image to which the dashing young man aspired. The car might have cost £45 in those halcyon days. Richard Habershon archives

But the Le Mans model was a hit and in an effort to broaden the market the chassis was extended to 118 inches to carry a full four-seat tourer body with the cycle fenders. The lengthened frame was not quite as rigid and the bodies deteriorated with flexing.

Summary and prospects

The improvements of the second series have attracted more collectors and values are stronger than for the first series. The Le Mans model is second only to the Ulster in desirability. Even shoddy examples can bring as much as £12,000, while tidy runners should be worth £16,000. Nicely restored examples begin around £23,000, while super specimens can reach £35,000. The high-radiator standard models do not have the following of the low-chassis models and are worth much less. Few cars appear in the public market and sales are most often found through club sources. Appreciation should be steady.

Forty-eight years later, Richard Habershon again sits in the seat of D2/203. The car's recent competition history is evident in the changes to wheels, tires, fenders and windscreen. There are some changes in the driver, too, but he seems ready to have another go! Richard Habershon archives

Chapter 4

1½ liter, third series; Mark II and Ulster

 ★★★★

January 1934-December 1935	
Production: 166 cars total	
2/4 seater	61
four seater	45
drophead coupe	8
Ulster	21
saloon	24
other	7

History

Both sales needs and substantial mechanical improvements suggested the introduction of a new model. The engine was given a new counterbalanced crankshaft and a reworked combustion chamber, and revs could then be taken into the 5000 rpm region. Horsepower was up to 73 with a 7.5:1 compression ratio. The frame was strengthened and the Hartford shocks were mounted transversely. The short chassis was now 103 inches and the long chassis, 120 inches.

Identification

The Mark II was fitted with vertical thermostatically controlled radiator shutters.

The famous Ulster LM 18, one of three Le Mans cars for 1935, which has had a distinguished racing history. The engine of this car has been steadily developed and current speeds of well over 100 mph substantially exceed the prewar specifications. Prices for good-to-superb examples are in the £30,000 to £50,000 range. Roger Stowers photo

The flexible exhaust pipes came through the hood (bonnet) sides. The two cowl humps were gone and the open cars had outside door handles. A clever idea was the use of the sidescreens as small racing visors (Brooklands screens), which could be raised when the windshield was folded flat.

Chassis numbers: A4/400/S to J4/468/S, J4/500/S to L5/596/L. Suffix U=Ulster, S=short, L=long. The prefix LM continues to indicate factory team cars.

Utility and performance

The Mark II was a smoother car than its predecessors and its performance was somewhat improved. The standard 2/4 seater could reach 60 mph from rest in twenty-two seconds and top speed reported by *The Autocar* was 84 mph. *Motor Sport* was able to reach 60 from rest in just under twenty seconds. The open four-seater was a bit slower but was able to show a top speed of over 80 mph.

These cars were heavy. The long-chassis saloon weighed over 2,800 pounds and its 0-60 time was around twenty-eight seconds with a top speed just over 75 mph.

This was not the case with the Ulster where meticulous attention to weight saving brought the all-up figure to just over 2,000 pounds. The 85 bhp engine, on a very high 9.5:1 compression, could push the Ulster to 100 mph and was so guaranteed. Contemporary developers of this model have raised horsepower and performance substantially.

Problem areas

The Mark II and, especially, the Ulster have been often used competitively and have proven to be tough cars, but breakage is possible in any component under stress. However, thanks to the resources of Morntane Engineering, strengthened parts for these engines and other areas have been manufactured which can produce durability equal to the best of modern practice. Rebuilds to these very high standards are expensive but owners are secure in the knowledge that help and spares are readily available.

The engine of LM 18 originally produced 85 bhp at 5250 rpm. Progressive development using modern internals has raised this figure to about 125 bhp. Roger Stowers photo

The long-chassis Mark II was not only roomy but had splendid instruments highlighted by the big speedometer and rev counter. Norman Herstein photo

Coachwork

The various body types are listed above. The long-chassis cars were subject to frame torsional flexing.

Summary and prospects

The Mark II series was the final and best expression of the original 1½ liter design and remains the preferred car of the series for those whose main interest is touring. The Le Mans model is still the choice of the buyer who intends to race as well. About eighty-one remain according to the Aston Martin Register but there are certainly more surviving. It would appear that all of the Ulsters are extant, though several are in a dismantled state.

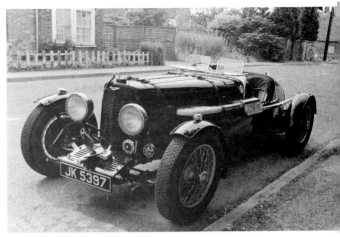

The Ulster was a purposeful car, a standout in the thirties. This view of 15/591/U shows the balance of the design. Roger Stowers archives

This drophead coupe, G4/461/L, was a very neat car but only eight examples were built. As a civilized personal sporting car, it would be had to beat. Roger Stowers photo

The long-chassis saloon found 24 buyers. This splendid example (LA/524/L), owned by Dudley Heath, is one of the few survivors. The weight of 2,815 pounds was a bit much for the 1½ liter engine, and performance required high revs in all gears. As a saloon design, however, it remains a masterpiece. Richard Habershon photo

The 10 foot wheelbase of the long-chassis Mark II provided sufficient room for a very low four-seater of which 61 were built. The tourer weighed 2,526 pounds which challenged the 1493 cc engine, even with 73 bhp at 4750 rpm. The rear end ratio was 4.66:1 which helped performance, but fast cruising demanded high revs. Prices for good examples are around £20,000. Norman Herstein photo

The demand for the Mark II is strong. Prices for poor specimens start around £12,000 and go steadily upward to about £30,000. The rare saloons on the long chassis are worth around £20,000. Steady though slow appreciation may be expected.

The Ulster prices are the highest of all the prewar cars, with ordinary examples fetching £30,000 and more. Pristine examples in fully developed and rebuilt state can top £60,000.

The narrow frontal appearance of the Mark II was enhanced by the cylce-type fenders which also reduced drag. Dean Batchelor photo

The typical and very handsome 2/4 seater body was fitted to 61 of the Mark II models. Prices for these cars in good condition are in the £20,000 to £30,000 range. Dean Batchelor photo

The low-sweeping lines of the long-chassis tourer are emphasized in this photograph. Norman Herstein photo

Rarely has saloon coachwork been mated to a cycle-fendered sporting chassis with such good effect. This car, K4/513/L, is one of the few remaining examples. Roger Stowers photo

Chapter 5

Two-liter; Speed model, 15/98 and C type

★
★★Speed models

```
August 1936-August 1940
Production:   approximately 171 cars total
(including two works prototypes)
    Abbey 2/4 seater                      48
    Abbey drophead coupe                   1
    Abbott of Farnham drophead coupe      25
    Bertelli long saloon                  51
    Bertelli long drophead coupe           1
    Speed model (9 Bertelli, 2 Abbey,
    C7/719/U)                             12
    C type Speed model                     8
    Bertelli long-chassis tourer          24
    Proto Ex600                            1
```

History

By 1935 the 1½ liter model was in trouble on two counts: It was very expensive and it was having a hard time coping with growing weight. Though two other proprietary engines were considered along with a radical innovation, the cross rotary valve engine (See Inman Hunter, *Aston Martin 1914 to 1940: A Pictorial Review*, page 150), the simplest solution was to bore the Mark II engine out to about two liters. The precise volume was 1949 cc. On a 7.75:1 compression ratio, the brake horsepower jumped at once to ninety-eight. About fifteen Speed model chassis were built with dry-sump lubrication, but production centered on a new wet-sump version.

Though the short-chassis wheelbase was slightly reduced to ninety-nine inches, the overall length went up by almost two feet, caused principally by overhang of the sweeping fenders at the rear. Girling hydraulic brakes were fitted and the car had adjustable rear shock absorbers. The cycle fenders were mounted on the chassis and no longer turned with the wheels.

The touring models were mounted on a 116-inch-wheelbase long chassis. Though Aston Martins were still very expensive, prices were reduced in 1938, the tourers costing £475.

Identification

The two-liter Astons were bulkier than the earlier cars. Sweeping fender lines marked all the touring models. The cycle fenders of the rare Speed models were attached to the frame. The wet-sump engine was fitted to the touring models.

Chassis numbers: G6/701/UR to E8/874/SO. First letter=month, first number=year (G6=June 1936).

Performance and utility

The new cars had a more powerful engine, but their weight was climbing sharply. The simple 2/4 tourer weighed 2,800 pounds while the saloon was over 3,100 pounds. Frontal area was up. Though acceleration was improved, 0-60 about twenty seconds, top speed was just over 80 mph for the open cars. The rear axle ratio was still 4.67:1, which meant that the new engine, both bored and stroked, was working with higher loads at top revs. The car seems to like cruising at about 55 mph though early road tests spoke of cruising at 70 and 80 mph. Hydraulic brakes are a great improvement despite the objections of the purists.

This rare two-liter saloon was a well-built car with all of the Aston Martin quality features. However, the weight of 3,100 pounds was too much for the 98 hp engine. The styling of the saloon was undistinquished and inferior to the Jaguar and the big MGs which sold at about half the price. Only five were sold, in part because the engine was too rough for closed coachwork. Roger Stowers photo

The Speed model could touch 100 mph, but an 8.3:1 compression and a 4.4 axle ratio were necessary. On balance the two-liter was a much more "modern" car both in appearance and driving feel, which may have added utility. Enthusiasts moaned the loss of the old cycle fender "look" and the spartan accommodations.

Luxury touches included the Jackall hydraulic jacking system. Synchromesh gears on the top three ratios of the Moss box were a further refinement, again probably not welcomed by enthusiasts.

Problem areas

Teething troubles with the two-liter included general roughness of the engine. Early engines with the Specialloid pistons had a habit of seizing. A vibration period, usually around 1500 rpm, was never fully solved. Engine troubles were sufficiently serious that the factory was preparing to replace the sohc units with the new pushrod two-liter developed during the war. Five prewar cars were so fitted.

Only eight C type roadsters were built. The streamlined look was not well received by Aston enthusiasts and the last car sold in 1940. On the plus side, the reduction in drag was substantial and the C type would do 100 mph. The more conventionally bodied Speed models will be worth more but as a rare curiosity, the C type is highly collectible and performance is near the top of the prewar Aston Martin models. Roger Stowers photo

It should be remembered that the two-liter engines were bored-out versions of the 1½ liter unit, which means that at the present time rebuilds require great care because the cylinders will not tolerate more than a 0.030 inch overbore, and liners may be necessary.

Axle tramp was cured by the fitting of Wilmot-Breedon harmonic stabilizing bumpers, a common palliative on many makes including Rolls-Royce and Bentley. The engine problem was not so quickly cured, so production was shifted away from saloon bodies which emphasized the roughness. This eventually cost the company a break with body supplier Harry Bertelli.

Coachwork

Bertelli's bodies for the two-liter touring cars have not aged well. The car stood very much higher than the 1½ liter series and had lost that lovely low racy look. An exception is the two-liter Ulster model which was close in appearance to the 1½ liter body.

The C type, which first appeared in the 1938 model year, was a very rounded roadster body mounted on unsold Speed model chassis. Eight were built and sold but the last did not sell until July 1940, despite the war and shortage of cars. The C type brought a reduction of drag which enabled the two-liter to achieve 100 mph.

Abbotts of Farnham built a drophead coupe on the short chassis, which is a bit truncated though certainly better looking than the saloon.

The new bulk of the two-liter bodies meant that much of the sheet metal was now farther from direct frame support; as

At the 1966 Horsfall meet, the 1925 GP car competed against a two-liter tourer. The two-liter series was generally heavy looking but in this light-bodied form it was a pretty car. Prices for the two-liter have been modest. Edward Negus photo from Derrick Edwards archives

a result, the bodies can show the usual decay so common in post-vintage cars. Doors can sag and sheet metal can crack.

Summary and prospects

The two-liter cars have not attracted many enthusiasts; as a result, the market prices are much lower than for other prewar units. This has slowed restoration and investment of these models. Many appear on the market in unrestored or downright dilapidated condition. Their prices are low and this further drags down the prices on really good specimens. There is little demand for the saloons.

Asking prices may start at £3,000 for poor examples of the saloon, while the top of this market appears to be about £10,000. Open

The late Malcolm Cann's 1937 15/98 two-liter, F7/808/U, a neat 2/4 seater by Abbey coachworks. The two-liter not only looks right in this form but goes well and this particular car has had a long competition history. Roger Stowers photo

A 1938 15/98 two-liter, G8/827/SO, with Abbey 2/4 seater coachwork. This model should bring strong prices in the two-liter class. Roger Stowers photo

coachwork on a fine example may bring £16,000 or more.

Perhaps no more than half of the 173 cars appear to have survived, of which nine are Speed models and three are C type Speed models. The Speed models are much more valuable and their high rate of survival attests to the better opinion enthusiasts have of them. A true two-liter Ulster again may bring very high prices, around the £50,000 level.

The Spa Special, J6/707/U, a two-liter Speed model which was originally a 2/4 seater by Bertelli. It was used as a works demonstrator. This car was driven in the 1949 24 hours at Spa (Horsfall, fourth and second in class). It was owned for many years by the Freeman family and is still winning races. Roger Stowers photo

A Speed model two-liter which will be at the top of the market for this series. Roger Stowers photo

Chapter 6

Two-liter sports or DBl ★

September 1948-May 1950
Production: 14 cars total

History

David Brown purchased the Aston Martin firm in February 1947. On hand was a new 1970 cc pushrod ohv engine designed by Claude Hill which had been running in prototype form since 1944. The engine, though undeveloped, was of sound design and very tough. It gave 90 bhp at 4750 rpm. A new chassis had also been designed with independent front suspension by trailing links and coil springs. It had been tested during World War II by Hill in the form of an experimental saloon known as the Atom.

A special roadster constructed on these general principles was entered at Spa in 1948 and won, the new engine performing beautifully. With this splendid victory in hand, a small production run began. A Spa replica was cataloged.

The DB1, from this unusual angle, does indeed have some curious features. Note the registration plate (AM 1950), the folding windshield, the cutout rear wheel spats and the front fender "trunk." Not a great sports car, more a transitional model. Roger Stowers archives

Identification

Thirteen of the production cars were drophead coupes with very rounded lines, full-flowing fenders and a narrow central radiator flanked by two smaller grilled openings. The fourteenth car was a saloon which became a special.

Chassis numbers: AMC/48/1 to AMC/50/15.

Performance and utility

The production drophead weighed over 2,520 pounds with substantial frontal area. Acceleration was modest, with a top speed in the eighties. Girling twelve-inch hydraulic brakes were fitted.

Problem areas

The low production run of the DB1 has produced little service history. The Hill engine was a solid design, though undeveloped. The chassis was really the prototype for the DB2 and had many strong features.

Coachwork

The standard drophead coupe body was essentially a prewar design but was attractive.

Summary and prospects

The two-liter sports (DB1) was strictly an interim car produced while David Brown reorganized the company. The price with tax was £2,332 in 1949, while a Spa replica (for which there were no takers) was listed at £3,109! These prices put the Aston Martin into rare company and may be one reason few were sold. Perhaps half of the production cars survive and their appearance on the market is very rare. Without much performance and with an idiosyncratic style, the DB1 is unlike all other Aston Martins. However, as a curiosity, it will always retain interest though market prospects are uncertain, especially because spares are nonexistent.

Only 15 two-liter sports (or DB1) were built, and all have apparently survived. This is number AMC 48/2. The rather bulbous lines of the drophead coupes are emphasized by the photograph of a 1950 example. The 1970 cc engine developed by Claude Hill produced 90 bhp though its weight was over 2,500 pounds and increased frontal area did not help performance.

It may have been one of the reasons for the adoption of the Bentley-Watson six-cylinder unit for the DB2. Rarity has helped the value of these cars though they remain an interim enigma, neither prewar nor in the great postwar tradition which followed. Roger Stowers photo

Chapter 7

DB2

★★
★★★ Dropheads

May 1950-April 1953	
Production: 411 cars total	
saloon	309
drophead coupe	97
Graber drophead coupe	3
other ("tourer"?)	2

History

In 1948, David Brown bought the Lagonda company and set up the factory in Feltham. The new Lagonda LB6 was in prototype form with a 2.6 liter six-cylinder twin overhead cam engine designed by William Watson and W. O. Bentley. (A technical study of this engine may be found in Donald Bastow's *W. O. Bentley: Engineer*, chapter 13.)

For the 1949 Le Mans race, three new Aston Martins were prepared with striking new coupe bodies designed by Frank Feeley. Two of these cars had the Claude Hill four-cylinder engine, the third had the 2.6 liter Lagonda engine. This last represents the true prototype of the DB2. It would be nice to say that it earned a first-year victory, as had the four-cylinder special at Spa the previous year, but the six-cylinder's water pump failed. However, at the 1949 Spa shortly afterward, this same car finished third overall, a promising beginning. (Andrew Whyte's *The Aston Martin and Lagonda*, volume 1, chapter 3 provides an excellent narrative history and pictures on this model.)

Identification

The familiar Aston Martin shape was first seen in the beautiful coupe body. The whole front of the car hinged forward to provide access to the engine and front suspension. The short ninety-nine-inch wheelbase of the DB2 was accentuated by the 600x16 inch tires.

The serial numbers are as follows:
LMA/49/1 to 4, the three early team cars and a development car
LML/50/5 to 406 (cars up to number 49 have three-piece grilles and side vents)
LML/50/X1 to X5

It is important to check the engine number to determine which of the several versions is fitted. The numbers and specifications are as follows:
LB6B, 6.5:1 compression, 105 bhp at 5000 rpm (the early engine)
LB6E, 7.5:1 compression, 116 bhp at 5000 rpm
LB6V, the "Vantage" engine, 8.16:1 compression, 125 bhp (January 1951)
VB6B, a big-valve Vantage engine
VB6E, the VB6B fitted to export (E) models with modified controls

Performance and utility

The DB2 began a totally new performance

image for the Aston Martin. A low weight of 2,453 pounds with 105 bhp in a sleek coupe body produced a maximum speed of 116 mph in an early *The Motor* test and a top of 110 mph by *The Autocar*. Zero-to-sixty times were 11.2 and 12.4 respectively for the two magazines. (*The Aston Martin: A Collection of Contemporary Road Tests 1948-1959*, compiled by Adrian Feather, provides seven road tests, including two reports by Phil Hill and one by John Bolster.)

The trailing-link suspension was a revelation when the DB2 appeared. Handling appeared unaffected by road camber. The high average speeds were astonishing for a car of only 2.6 liters.

Phil Hill was ecstatic about his new DB2 and reported in *Road & Track* averaging over 80 mph for two hours on a Reno trip, and this with the normal engine. Even with the 2.6 engine at lowest specified power, the light weight of the DB2 gave this first model of the David Brown series a more sporting feeling than later cars.

Problem areas

The DB2 engines were low-stressed and should last a long time given decent maintenance. Crankshaft trouble is rare, but be on the lookout for engines with oil pressures below fifty pounds hot. Replacement crankshafts are very difficult to find.

A problem sometimes encountered is leakage of the head gasket. The cylinder liners fit tightly together between cylinders 1 and 2, 3 and 4, and 5 and 6, with very little surface to present to the gasket. The gasket is very narrow. But the problem is compounded because the tops of the liners must be in an absolutely flat plane.

Setting up the liners requires that they project above the top of the block so that when the head is tightened, a good and consistent seal is obtained. Unfortunately,

The fourth development car, LML/49/4, was raced by the factory in 1950. The radiator grille was very low and the side louvers were of the earliest pattern. The coupe body was smaller than the production version. The front bumper was little more than a trim strip which matched the side trim at the rocker panels. Air scoops were cut into the rear windows. This picture is dated May 1949. Roger Stowers photo

An early DB2, LML/50/5, with the grille that was evolved from the DB1 and used in the first 49 production cars. The Claude Hill two-liter pushrod engine was initially fitted in this particular car but the chassis soon became a test bed for the six-cylinder engine. The side vent was a refinement from the prototype cars and, like the early grille, was dropped after the forty-ninth car. The front bumper, still no more than a trim strip, was divided to allow the mounting of the license plate. Roger Stowers photo

the liners are not always of the same length nor is the base of the block on which they rest in a uniform plane, so gaskets are available in various thicknesses to produce an equal projection of all six liners. This is a delicate and tedious fitting procedure.

Even if the liners project precisely the same distance (0.004 inch) the problem may not be entirely solved. Some suggest that the liners may expand at unequal rates when there is spot heating, a result in part of the build up of muck. Liners 1 and 6 run generally cooler but the adjacent internal liners, 2 and 5, may expand more and compromise the delicate gasket sealing.

The lesson of all of this is that an engine rebuild must be done completely and expertly. Engines that are accurately set up rarely have gasket trouble. The DB2 engine does not tolerate halfway measures.

The drophead coupe appeared in late 1950 and shared the small lid of the saloons. The two rear windows were a nice vintage touch which also reduced the chance of breakage when folding. Photo by Louis Klemantaski from Roger Stowers archives

The trim strip was continued around the back of the car on the DB2. A small lid allowed access to the spare tire. The rear window was narrow and was an instant identification of the early cars from the rear. Roger Stowers photo

The production DB2s looked like this with the redesigned grille. The trim strip was gone from the rocker panels which tended to lower the appearance of the car. It is easy to see why this magnificent design caught the fancy of enthusiasts. Good examples may be found in the $10,000 area with top specimens up to $20,000. Roger Stowers photo

Phil Hill recalled another curious problem. The chain tensioner depends on oil pressure; if an engine has a stretched chain and is given an oil change followed by a start-up with momentary lack of pressure, the chain can jump a sprocket causing a timing change or much worse. An oil pressure failure due to other causes can therefore be dangerous to more than bearings.

Buyers should examine oil to see if there is any of the familiar creamy emulsion caused by water and also check the radiator for oil in the water. Sometimes an emulsion will

The four-main-bearing DB2 engine was designed by William Watson and Walter O. Bentley for the Lagonda. The very deep crankcase extended well below the centerline of the crankshaft for rigidity, a feature made possible by mounting the main bearings in cylindrical housings or "cheeses" which were fed into the block from the rear. This eliminated the oil leakage at the mains which no longer had to seal to both crankcase and sump. At a 6.5 compression, the 2.6 liter engine produced 105 bhp. When carefully set up, these engines are reliable and long lasting. Roger Stowers photo

The trailing-link suspension of the DB2 provided a vertical rise and fall of the front wheels. The oil reservoir in the front cross tube is sometimes overlooked in servicing, with bad consequences. When properly maintained, however, these early front ends are long lasting. Roger Stowers photo

The very compact appearance of the early drophead is emphasized in this picture. There is virtually no space at all behind the rear seat.

Only 102 were built and they remain very desirable automobiles. Roger Stowers photo drip on the garage floor that has nothing to do with the head gasket. This could be the result of water and oil combining in the open space between the water pump and the chain case through which a shaft passes. There are two seals, one for water and one for oil, and both tend to leak into the draining space.

Hard driving will take its toll on tires and clutches. It has been suggested that clutch life can be as short as 10,000 miles under severe use (!) or as long as 25,000 miles under favorable circumstances. Noncompetitive driving should produce much higher mileages. It should be noted that first gears are no longer available for the David Brown gearbox; some noise can be expected. The early Salisbury rear axles occasionally give trouble, and shock loading should be avoided. The new bodies reduced air circulation around the brakes, so fade is likely. Unless maintenance is steady and care is used in driving, all of these items may be short-lived.

The DB2 and DB2/4 instrument panels used four round instrument and switch panels which were derived from the prewar Lagonda. They were handsome, legible and symmetrical. Roger Stowers photo

The box tube chassis construction was strong and light, and served well until the end of the DB MkIII series. Roger Stowers photo

The trailing-link front suspension is often ignored by owners. A large aluminum housing is filled with oil which in time may leak. Even worse is the possibility that someone has jacked the car under this housing, which could have distorted it and caused leakage. The steering box has a cork gasket which may allow the gears to run dry. This will increase free play at the steering wheel and, if ignored, cause a breakup of bearings. The repair of the front suspension is very expensive; a careful examination should be made.

A total engine overhaul to the highest standards may cost about $10,000.

Coachwork

The beauty of the DB2 elicited everyone's admiration. Finish and, especially, interior layout were superb. The four big circular instrument and switch clusters still fascinate.

The drophead coupe version appeared in late 1950 and ninety-seven were made out of the total production. These very handsome open cars are much sought after. Three dropheads were also built by Graber and two other chassis were fitted with special bodies.

Summary and prospects

The early DB2s languished for many years and were frequently rescued from oblivion at near-junk prices. Low power when compared to later versions was one obstacle. But the charm of these early cars has found new favor and has drawn the attention of Aston Martin enthusiasts. Operating costs are relatively low and performance is excellent. Prices have been climbing steadily. The top of the DB2 market is about $20,000. More usual prices for good examples are in the $10,000 region, with running but poor specimens starting around $4,000. The very early three-piece-grille models with side venting are much sought after and may be worth more. Drophead DB2s are commanding prices approximately fifty percent higher than coupe versions.

The second DB2, chassis LMA/49/2, was one of the two team cars with the Claude Hill 1970 cc engine. In 1949 it finished seventh overall at Le Mans and fifth at Spa. Here it is being driven by Whitehouse in the two-liter production race at Silverstone in May 1951. In this racing trim the car is "all business." The taut body design was revolutionary at the time. T. C. March photo

Chapter 8

DB3

★★★★

September 1951-May 1953
Production: 10 cars total

History

The DB3 was developed in 1950 and 1951 for competition purposes and is only somewhat related to the general specification of the production cars. The ladder frame with torsion bars is an echo of Auto Union practice, to be expected from designer Eberan von Eberhorst. Andrew Whyte points out that von Eberhorst also worked on the Jowett Jupiter which was related to this type of frame construction. A de Dion rear suspension was new for Aston Martin.

The engine was initially the 2.6 Vantage unit, which was tuned to 140 bhp with the use of three Weber carburetors and the 8.16:1 compression. A 2.9 liter engine was fitted and used in some of the cars beginning at Monaco in 1952; it eventually produced 163 bhp.

The racing record of the five DB3 factory cars was mixed, with a win at the Goodwood 9 Hours in 1952 being their best moment. Some DB3s, such as DB3/5, have continued to be strongly competitive in recent club events.

Identification

There were only ten cars of this series produced, of which eight survive.

Chassis numbers: DB3/1 to DB3/10. An original engine will have a number beginning with DP/101.

Performance and utility

The DB3 was a racing car and as such cannot be measured from a utilitarian standpoint. Performance is directly related to tune and other nonclassifiable factors.

Coachwork

The standard body was a roadster with an egg-crate grille with large spaces. Two coupes were built and there have been several body switches and rebuilds.

Problem areas

The specialized nature and intense use of the DB3 require high maintenance. Mechanical failures are part of the racing game. There have been some engine swaps along the way in several cars.

Summary and prospects

As an exotic racing car, the DB3 commands high value. Its competitive position, however, is overshadowed by the much more successful DB3S. Originality counts in the occasional DB3 displayed in concours or at racing shows. Owners rarely part with these cars—direct contact through

Here is DB3/4, the third of four team cars and one of the eight surviving DB3s. This car had a busy factory-supported competition history in 1952 and 1953 but did not score any major victories. George Abecassis is shown in practice at Silverstone, May 1952. A fine DB3 may have a value around £45,000. T. C. March photo

Lance Macklin drove this DB3/5 to fourth place at the Silverstone meeting in 1952. Later in the season, this car was holding fourth place at Le Mans when it retired after 20 hours. In 1953 it placed second at the Sebring 12 Hour. T. C. March photo

the AMOC roster is the only way to investigate availability. There is no "market" in the normal sense. Prices for ordinary examples will be about £30,000, with top specimens at £45,000.

DB3/2, the only DB3 built with full road equipment with full-width windshield. At one time this car served as personal transport for David Brown. Roger Stowers photo

DB3/7, a one-off coupe used by David Brown's daughter, Angela. Roger Stowers photo

DB3/8, a production DB3 still looking fairly
original except for the windshield. This car was
at Le Mans in 1985. Roger Stowers photo

Chapter 9

DB2/4

★★
★★★ Dropheads

October 1953-October 1955
Production: 565 cars total

History

Various modifications of the DB2 took place in 1953 to enlarge the interior and provide two very small occasional seats. The car was first presented at the London Motor Show in 1953. The 2.6 liter engine was enlarged to 2922 cc in April 1954.

Identification

The extended roofline with larger rear window and longer rear "fender" development gave the DB2/4 a sense of bulk not found in the DB2. The one-piece curved windshield replaced the two pieces found on the DB2. True bumpers with guards set away from the body gave much-needed protection, as compared to the very simple strips fitted directly to the DB2 body.

Chassis numbers: LML/501 to LML/1065. The 2.6 Vantage engine used in the DB2 was initially fitted with engine code number VB6E. The 2.9 liter engine numbers begin with VB6J.

Performance and utility

Top speed for the 2.9 engined DB2/4 was 118 mph with 0-60 mph times reported as low as under eleven seconds by *The Motor*.

The tractability of the engine was noticed by all testers, and the DB2/4 is entirely usable for mundane around-town work.

There is very little ventilation in the closed cars, and the construction of some sort of extraction system by vents is helpful. The rear windows of the later DB MkIII were hinged, which helped.

Coachwork

Both the closed and drophead versions were offered from the beginning. There were approximately seventy-three drophead bodies built. Eight others were fitted with Bertone bodies, and there were a very few more with bespoke coachwork.

Problem areas

The general comments in Chapter 7 on the DB2 also apply to the DB2/4.

Overheating can be another common problem on almost all models. A good hard run and a warmish day should give indication if trouble is ahead. Assuming that all of the usual checks have been made and the radiator is clean, more subtle problems can be present. Muck can build up around the liners which can hasten spot heating, which could cause liner expansion and gasket leakage. If the gasket does leak, it will usually cause heating through direct firing of the water by the charge and also by forcing water out of the system. Water pumps have been known to fail.

Summary and prospects

The DB2/4 enjoys the same market conditions as the DB2. Prices start around $4,000, with nice specimens showing up at $10,000 and up. The 2/4 remains a favorite for those who like the four circular panels for instruments and switchwork on the dashboard. As these cars age and restoration costs rise, the market should slowly appreciate. Dropheads in good shape should bring $15,000 or more.

The inviting interior was all "business." The beautiful instruments were not rearranged, however, for the left-hand-drive version, and the tachometer remains on the extreme right, out of the driver's normal field of vision. Louis Klemantaski photo

The "4" in the DB2/4 meant four seats, perhaps an optimistic specification when first viewed by the entering rear passenger. Interior finish and fit was of the highest quality. Louis Klemantaski photo

The DB2/4 was given an extended roofline and larger rear windows. The rear deck lid was much enlarged and included the rear window. Proper bumpers were fitted, including guards. The sheet metal that supported the former bumper strips was still visible. The one-piece windshield enhanced the smoothness of the design. Good examples of these cars should be found around $10,000. Louis Klemantaski photo

The front seat cushions and backs were rather flat and did not give much lateral support, though few complained. The high door sills were required by the design of the tubular frame. Roger Stowers photo

The standard drophead continued on the 2/4 and 73 were built. Now and then a chassis made its way to a private coachbuilder. This particular car was built by Hermann Graber in Switzerland and has the usual Graber touches as seen in the windshield design, seat pleating, rear fender design and door latches. The grille is not unlike the very early DB2. Specialist-built Astons like this one will likely bring premium prices. Roger Stowers photo

speed and comfort on long-distance touring

The DB2/4 is at once identified by the real bumpers, instead of the trim strips fastened directly to the sheet metal as on the DB2. The guards or overriders were optional. Roger Stowers archives

A specially bodied convertible by Touring of Milan was built for Eric Vernon Rowe, editor of *Classic and Sports Car*. This car was one of two and was sold in 1983 for £22,000. Frank Dale photo

This DB2/4 went out to Hong Kong in 1955 and returned to England ten years later with only 50,000 km. Drophead coupes bring strong prices, especially with low mileage. Frank Dale photo

Chapter 10

DB3S   ★ ★ ★ ★ ★

May 1953-December 1956
Production: 30 cars total
(including 19 production models)

History

The DB3S was a completely redesigned competition car which, as a factory entry, was raced thirty-five times—it won fifteen times, was second thirteen times, and was third seven times. In private hands these splendid cars continue to be raced in club events with success. Detailed specifications may be found in the Aston Martin Register. In brief, the 2922 cc engine was given substantial development, and maximum brake horsepower by 1955 was 240 at 6000 rpm. Many features were tried experimentally, including inboard disc rear brakes from the DB3, twin-plug aluminum heads, superchargers, three-plate clutches, wishbone front suspension and CAV fuel injection.

The production cars used an 8.68:1 compression with a single-plug cast-iron head and three Weber 40 DC03 carburetors giving an output of 180 bhp at 5500 rpm. The clutch was hydraulically operated.

Identification

Buyers of these rare cars will presume to receive full competition history and details of modifications from the sellers.

Chassis numbers begin with DB3S. Original engine numbers of the production cars begin with VB6K. The factory team racing cars have engine numbers beginning with DP101.

Performance and utility

The DB3S accelerated from 0-60 in 6.6 seconds and touched 140 mph. It is remarkable that the DB4 as a standard touring car equaled this top speed only three or four years later and, in GT form, equaled the acceleration. Nevertheless, as an under-three-liter car, the DB3S remains a magnificent achievement and was the most successful Aston Martin competition effort to that time.

Problem areas

Owners of these great cars who use them in competition do not shrink from major and costly rebuilds of all components.

Coachwork

Three of the production cars were coupes; the rest were open roadsters. There have been numerous modifications to many of these cars over the years.

Summary and prospects

Those interested in vintage racing could do little better than invest in a DB3S. These cars are lovingly cared for by their owners and many continue to compete with success. Since the value of a racing car depends so much upon its given condition at any particular moment, estimates of value are difficult. But it is safe to say that no DB3S in complete form will be sold for under £50,000. Original examples that have not been heavily rebuilt will bring up to £90,000. Team cars with twin-plug heads, racing Borrani wheels and a good history are worth much more—usually in six figures.

DBS3/102 was actively raced in Australia for many years. These tough and very fast cars were competitive in private venues long after production ceased. Beautiful examples now bring six-figure dollar prices. Derrick Edwards archives

Only three DB3S coupes were built, of which this is the survivor. The other two, which were team cars, crashed at Le Mans in 1954. Paul Laub photo

DB3S/101 has been campaigned for many years with success. There were three general body styles for the production cars, of which this car is an example of the second. These cars are so rare that even well-used examples are rarely below $100,000. Paul Laub photo

Here Peter Collins is heading for third place in the British Grand Prix meeting at Silverstone in July 1953. The car is DB3S/2, the second team car, and is representative of the original style. Apart from Le Mans, the first-season record was excellent, with a fine string of victories. Prices for these cars begin at £50,000. T. C. March photo

The egg-crate grille is gone and there are other subtle sheet metal changes on the DB3S/7 which began life as a coupe but was rebodied after a crash at Le Mans in 1954. Roy Salvadori is on his way to a win at Aintree in 1955. Horsepower was 240 with 0-60 mph times just over six seconds. T. C. March photo

A second air scoop has now appeared on the right side of DB3S/5, here driven by Stirling Moss in 1956. This was the last year of factory

competition for this car but it has carried on very well in club events. T. C. March photo

Two more team cars which would become very well known, DB3S/6 and DB3S/7. These two were originally built as coupes but were re-bodied after the Le Mans crash in 1954. Roger Stowers photo

DB3S/5 shows some of the superb body design work of Frank Feeley. Roger Stowers photo

One of 20 production cars and the last one made, DB3S/120, which has been owned by Victor Gauntlett. It is one of only three fixed-head coupes. Roger Stowers photo

Team car DB3/S with an unusual head fairing. Roger Stowers photo

Chapter 11

DB2/4 MkII

★★
★★★ Dropheads

October 1955-August 1957	
Production: 199 cars total	
saloon	139
drophead coupe	24
fixed head coupe	34
spider by Touring	2

History

A refined DB2/4 using the by-then-standardized 2922 cc VB6J engine was first offered for the 1956 season. There were many detail improvements, some of which may be used for identification. Be on the lookout for engines numbered VB6J/—/L and VB6J/—/L1 with big valves and a high-lift cam producing 165 bhp. An 8.6:1 compression piston was also available.

Identification

Chassis numbers begin with a new prefix, AM300/1101 to AM300/1299. A fly-off hand brake replaced the umbrella pull. The lower part of the front fender was fixed and did not open with the hood. A kick-open air vent was fitted to this panel on each side. The bodies were made by Tickford, acquired by David Brown in 1955. Coachwork badges may be found just ahead of the front door pillar. The chrome-plated trim strip beneath the windows was extended around the rear of the car in a horizontal plane.

Performance and utility

Performance with the standard engine was perhaps fractionally better than the DB2/4, probably because a 3.77 axle ratio was used instead of a 3.73 but the difference was very small. The many improvements included such nice touches as courtesy switches for interior lights and improved seats. With each passing model the Aston Martin became more civilized, lamented perhaps by some, but applauded by more.

Problem areas

The summary in Chapter 7 on the DB2 also applies to the DB2/4 MkII.

Coachwork

The bodies, now built at Tickford, were beautifully finished as always. The new notch-backed fixed-head coupe was a nice addition.

Summary and prospects

The DB2/4 MkII was the last Aston Martin to have the wonderful row of circular dials on the instrument panel. It was also the last model which directly related in specification to the original DB2. The comparative rarity of this model has made it a target for some collectors, and the market for this particular model will remain strong. Prices should be about the same as for the DB2/4.

The DB2/4 MkII had numerous minor changes. A particularly noticeable one is a chrome strip which passed all the way around the car under the rear window. Chrome molding also marked the break in the fixed front fender, the hood opening above it. Roger Stowers photo

Chapter 12

DB MkIII ★★★

March 1957-July 1959
Production: 551 cars total

History

The final refinement of the early Feltham DB cars was the excellent MkIII, which in chassis specification was very similar to the DB2/4 MkII. However, Girling front disc brakes were available as an option from the beginning and were standardized after the first 100 cars. These superb brakes were also used on the DB4GT and later V8s.

The engine was heavily reworked by Tadek Marek, the gifted engineer who had recently joined Aston Martin from Austin. The strength of many components was increased, beginning with the block and crankshaft. Performance was up thanks to manifold redesign, large valves and a high-lift camshaft. Higher-output versions became available.

An overdrive was offered which reduced the rear axle ratio from 3.77 to 2.93, though normally a 4.09 ratio was recommended which would then give an overdrive ratio of 3.18:1.

Identification

The MkIII had a new smoother grille which was more vertical and very attractive. The instrument cluster was new and positioned directly in front of the driver.

Chassis numbers: AM300/3A/1300 to AM300/3/1850.

A careful check of engine numbers may reveal or verify examples of the special-tuned versions.

DBA, 162 bhp at 5500 rpm, the standard engine, twin SU carburetors, 8.16 compression (with twin exhausts, 178 bhp)

DBB, 195 bhp with three Weber 35 DC0 or three SU carburetors, 8.68 compression (ten cars)

DBD, 180 bhp with two or three SU carburetors (forty-seven cars)

DBC, 214 bhp (one car, a highly tuned special)

The disc brakes on most of the MkIIIs are easily visible behind the front wheel spokes.

Performance and utility

The MkIII was faster than the MkII despite a weight of over 2,800 pounds, and power was sharply up. Zero-to-sixty times fell below ten seconds. With any of the tuned engine versions, top speed was over 123 mph and 0-60 times fell to about 8.5 seconds. The brakes were much better. The interior layout was more driver oriented, from the fine instrument cluster to the new gearshift lever.

Problem areas

The general comments on the DB2 engine, Chapter 7, also apply here.

The reworking of the 2922 cc engine by Marek solved the problem of the liner level on the block. Liners were now seated at the top which meant heat no longer could cause expansion up the full length of the liner, a possible cause of trouble according to some owners. Furthermore, the tedious fitting of shims at the base of the liners to produce equal heights was eliminated. Integrity of the head gasket was improved.

A new feature was introduced in the liners: three lands at the base containing an O-ring at top and bottom with the empty middle land draining to the side of the block through a weep hole. Water from the top or oil from the bottom working its way past the O-rings would thus be evident through the weep holes. If such is the case, the engine may need an early overhaul. Owners have been known to block these weep holes. This dangerous practice would, at worst, drive water down into the sump. Check the weep holes carefully.

MkIII heads are in short supply. The two main problems are heads cracking and valve seats wearing. There are no hard seats on the head surfaces and, with repeated grinding, the valves lower into the head. If an engine overheats, examine the head carefully. Heads may be reconditioned and hard seats installed but at substantial cost.

The water pump was improved on the MkIII and was further developed after chassis number AM300/3B/1401.

Coachwork

The three bodies of the DB2/4 MkII were continued: the swept-back saloon, the notchback coupe and the drophead coupe.

The DB MkIII front disc brake caliper was barely visible behind the spokes. Roger Stowers photo

Summary and prospects

Many Aston Martin enthusiasts regard the DB MkIII as the most desirable of the early-series Feltham cars, certainly in mechanical development and styling perfection. Prices have been slightly stronger than for the DB2/4. As the last expression of the original David Brown design, the MkIII retains the sports car "feel" as opposed to the GT "feel" which would characterize the DB4.

Prices for the poorest examples will be in the $5,000 range, while nice specimens may be found at around $12,000 and up. Drophead coupes will have the usual fifty percent premium, maybe more on this model.

The DB MkIII engine had many changes from the earlier engines, including better sealing and positioning of the cylinder liners. The three-liter engine produced 162 bhp in the DBA version with 195 bhp available in the DBB with triple Weber carburetors. Roger Stowers photo

The new instrument panel layout, positioned either on left or right, established themes that lasted through the DB6. Tach and speedometer were directly in front of the driver. Roger Stowers photo

The DB MkIII was the final refined statement of the original DB2, and a very beautiful car it was. The new grille lowered the hoodline at the front. The rear windows opened, which improved ventilation. This model has found many followers. Ralph Poole/Dean Batchelor photo

The interior was trimmed to a very high standard. However, the seat cushions and backs were still flat and offered no lateral support. Instruments were grouped directly in front of the driver in a pattern that continued through the DB6. Dean Batchelor archives

The spare wheel was neatly stowed under the trunk and was quickly reached. Luggage remained undisturbed. Dean Batchelor archives

The rear deck lid opening was very large and the interior floor was neatly finished with ribbed rubber and chrome outline strips on the folding seatbacks. Roger Stowers photo

The fullness in the rear roofline was characteristic of the early cars, and on the MkIII it was typical. The balance of this great design was evident from any angle. The MkIII was certainly the most refined of the pre-DB4 cars. Prices for good clean saloons should be around $12,000 and up. Dean Batchelor archives

The DB MkIII drophead coupe is much desired and will bring prices often 50 percent higher than closed cars. This lovely example was shown at the 1985 Greenwich Nautical College concours. Roger Stowers photo

One of the rare notchback coupes, number
AM300/3/1830, on the DB MkIII chassis. Roger
Stowers photo

Chapter 13

DBR

★ ★ ★ ★ ★

1956-1960
Production: 14 cars total

History

The DBR series was initially designed for the 2½ liter Le Mans formula for 1956 and, though it retired, the design was sound. Successes began to appear in 1957, most notably at Spa and Nürburgring. The latter victory was repeated in 1958 and 1959. The greatest triumph was a one-two finish at Le Mans in 1959, overwhelming Jaguar and Ferrari—the winning team was Carroll Shelby and Roy Salvadori. At the close of the 1959 season, Aston Martin had won the World Sports Car Championship.

The DBR had various engines, including a version of the forthcoming 3.7 liter unit of the DB4. For a detailed history of this series see the Aston Martin Register and Andrew Whyte's fine narrative report, *The Aston Martin and Lagonda.*

Identification

Chassis numbers: DBR1/1 to DBR1/5, DBR2/1 to DBR2/2, DBR3/1, DBR4/1 to DBR4/4, DBR5/1 to DBR5/2. The first three

This DBR2/1 started in 1957 with a 3.7 liter engine, upped to 4.2 liters in 1958 when it came to the US as part of the Elisha Walker team. It was raced effectively by George Constantine and won the 1958 National Championship. The restoration included a complete new body built from photographs. DBRs bring the highest prices of all Aston Martins with values beginning in six figures. Ken Boyd archives

series are roadsters. The fourth and fifth series are single-seat grand prix cars. It appears that all have survived, apart from DBR3/1 which has become DBR1/4.

Performance and utility

These splendid competition cars had a brilliant racing record and surpassed all competition at their peak. Their utility has continued in club events.

Problem areas

These fine cars have proven very reliable. Substantial maintenance, rebuilding and so on are accepted from time to time by enthusiasts.

Coachwork

The open roadster bodies were not unlike the DB3S but the headlamps were covered and the bodies were generally

This DBR1/1 was driven by Salvadori at Aintree in July 1957. It was introduced at the end of the competitive life of the DB3S in 1956. The great advance in streamlining is obvious and, with lower drag, the car had much higher top speeds. DBR1/2 won Le Mans in 1959. The DBR4/1 began a series of single-seat Grand Prix cars which were entirely different in shape, though with an engine derived from the original DBR/1. T. C. March photo

cleaner. The single-seat GP cars are typical of the period.

Summary and prospects

The DBRs command very high prices. The Le Mans-winning car, DBR1/2, has a value of between £200,000 and £250,000, according to a recognized expert. Ordinary (if that term be used!) examples of this series should command a price of about £150,000.

Stirling Moss won the British Empire Trophy at Oulton Park in 1958 in the DBR2/1 with the 3.9 liter engine. Enthusiasts usually think of the DBR series as this classical shape. The DBR4, however, was a Grand Prix car with a single-seat open-wheel configuration. The engine of the GP car was derived from the 2.4 liter unit used in DBR1/1. Prices for the DBR in either GP or sports form are in six figures and a champion example such as the Le Mans-winning car could be worth $250,000. T. C. March photo

DBR1/2 in the back yard of the Hotel de France in La Chartre-sur-le-Loire, from whence it was driven to Le Mans by road where it won the race in 1959. This picture was taken in 1982. Roger Stowers photo

Only two DBR2s were made in 1957 and this is the second. It was driven by Moss at Nassau in December of 1959, the final appearance of a works-sponsored open Aston Martin in a sports car race. Roger Stowers photo

The single-seat DBR4, one of four GP cars quite unlike the first three DBR series. They first appeared in April 1959 and had a rather uncompetitive record. DBR4/1, here shown after an extensive rebuild, earned a second at Silverstone in 1959 driven by Salvadori. Roger Stowers photo

DBR4/4, the last of the four GP cars which was built as a spare and not raced by the works. It did have a long private career and has been seen in many historic races. Roger Stowers photo

Chapter 14

DB4

October 1958-June 1963	
Production: 1,110 cars total	
Series one	149
Series two	351
Series three	165
Series four (includes 30 dropheads)	260
Series five (includes 40 dropheads)	185

History

The new aluminum 3670 cc engine designed by Tadek Marek and tested in the DBR chassis was ready for series production in the late fifties. On an 8.25:1 compression ratio, this unit produced an advertised 240 bhp at 5500 rpm with twin SU HD8 carburetors (actually 208 bhp—the Corvette 427 of the period produced a true net of 297 bhp). The four-speed David Brown gearbox was used. The front suspension was changed to the more conventional unequal-wishbone system. At the rear, coil springs were used with a well-located conventional axle using parallel trailing links and Watts linkage. Dunlop disc brakes were fitted on all wheels but were replaced by Girlings in late production. Rack-and-pinion steering was used.

The superb new body was designed by Touring in Milan on a platform chassis using a tubular framework and was produced under license in the Tickford plant at Newport Pagnell. The Feltham days were drawing to a close; soon the company would center all production at Tickford. There were numerous production changes in both body and mechanical details.

The DB4 was first seen at the 1958 London Motor Show. The DB2/4 MkIII was not discontinued at that time and production of the two models overlapped until July 1959.

Identification

The AMOC devised a system for categorizing the DB4s; the factory did not use this system.

Series one—chassis numbers DB4/101/R to DB4/249/L, October 1958-February 1960. These early cars had the hood hinged at the rear. There were no bumper guards nor chrome window frames fitted to the first fifty cars. A fan cowl appeared on the last 100 cars.

Series two—chassis numbers DB4/250/L to DB4/600/R, January 1960-April 1961. The hood was hinged at the front. The sump had been increased from fifteen to seventeen pints. An oil cooler was fitted to thirty-three cars. Overdrive was first offered, usually with a higher axle ratio of 3.77 or even 4.09 (3.54 was standard).

Series three—chassis numbers DB4/601/R to DB4/765/R April 1961-September 1961. Electric tachometer, five rather than three demister outlets, triple-cluster taillights and two hood stays were fitted. Three of these cars had the 302 bhp GT engine (which was so stamped) and the latter two had separate engine-function gauges. After engine 370/571, a twenty-one-pint sump was fitted, an important change (see problem areas).

Series four—chassis numbers DB4/766/R to DB4/950/R Vantage "Saloons" DB4/951/R to DB4/995/R, convertibles DB4C/1051/R to DB4C/1080/L, September 1961-October 1962.

The most noticeable feature was the thinner air opening on the hood. The grille was new with seven vertical bars, a useful identifying feature. The ashtray sat on top of the gearbox instead of in the dash.

The special series (SS) or Vantage engine had a 9:1 compression and three SU carburetors, producing 266 bhp at 5750 rpm. It was first offered at chassis DB4/839/L. This engine was usually fitted in the DB4 Vantage, a chassis term which designated the restyled front with sloping headlamp covers like the DB4GT (and sometimes confused with the DB5). It is important to check the engine in any DB4 Vantage because it may not be an SS unit; similarly, SS engines may be found in standard cars. Oil coolers were normally fitted in series four production but some cars, even with SS engines, may not have them.

Five cars had the GT engine and a clue will be the separate gauges for engine functions, though seven standard cars also received the GT instruments. A wide-ratio gearbox was fitted to most cars after DB4/943/R. In it first and second gear were substantially lower, which eased the strain on the clutch.

Gear	Normal ratio	Wide ratio
4th	1:1	1:1
3rd	1.25:1	1.25:1
2nd	1.74:1	1.85:1
1st	2.49:1	2.92:1

The prototype DB4 with the familiar mesh grille. Bumper guards were fitted after the first 50 cars. The air scoop on the hood was enlarged and slightly rounded for production. Roger Stowers photo

The convertible was introduced at the London Motor Show in 1961 and there were thirty built in series four of which eleven had SS engines.

Series five—chassis numbers: saloons DB4/100/L to DB4/1050/R, convertibles DB4C/1081/L to DB4C/1110/L and DB4C/1166/R to DB4C/1175/L, Vantage saloons DB4/1111/R to DB4/1165/R and DB4/1176 to DB4/1215/L (but 1181, 1183, 1185 and 1187 had standard engines); September 1962-June 1963.

The series five car was lengthened about 3½ inches, to fifteen feet, which added both leg and luggage room. Fifteen-inch wheels were fitted for 6.70x15 tires (replacing 600x16). The roof was slightly higher, which alters the junction with the trunk lid. The revised instrument panel contained a full array of GT gauges with all functions separately dialed.

Apart from these first fifty saloons, most series five DB4s had the Vantage styling resembling the DB5 with the covered head-lamps. The SS engine was virtually standard after the first fifty saloons, though a few of the early cars were so fitted. Three series five cars had automatic transmission, and six Vantages had the GT engine.

Forty convertibles were built in series five and twenty-one had SS engines. Two convertibles, DB4C/1089/L and DB4C/1109/L, had the Vantage front end styling. One convertible, DB4C/1173/R, had a GT engine.

The DB4 was a handsome car, especially when measured on the tight, 98 inch wheelbase. The top speed of 140 mph was matched by precise handling and excellent four-wheel disc brakes. Aston Martin enthusiasts continue to hold this model in high regard. Because prices have been depressed by deteriorated examples, really good cars may still be found at bargain prices. Roger Stowers photo

Performance and utility

The DB4 marked a major step in the evolution of the Aston Martin as the car moved into the forefront of the great grand tourers. Both in size and weight, the car moved away from the earlier sporting characteristics of the DB2 and its successors. That part of the market would be catered to by the forthcoming DB4GT.

Top speed climbed to 140 mph and 0-60 time was around nine seconds. The four-wheel disc brakes were reassuring, though fade was possible under heavy use. Controls were heavy, especially the clutch and steering. General reliability and maintenance requirements were improved over the DB2/4 series.

A DB4 engine, properly overhauled, has a possible life of 100,000 miles under normal operating conditions. A proper overhaul means that the block and head are thoroughly heated for fitting of bearings, liners and guides, and that the appropriate special tools are used to avoid damage when dismantling and assembling. This is one reason Aston Martin engines are expensive to

rebuild. Owners prepared to maintain their cars to high standards will be rewarded by long service.

The factory will undertake to rebuild all used Aston Martins beginning with the DB4, an important resource for prospective buyers. Factory parts are available.

Coachwork

The closed body, as created by Touring, was a lasting design and identified the basic Aston Martins until the DBS. The convertible (drophead) coupe was equally attractive with a top or hoodline that showed a beautiful economy of line similar to the other Touring bodies, such as that fitted on the Lancia Flaminia and on the 3500GT Maserati.

Problem areas

The several modifications to the engine in the early series pointed up a singular problem: The new aluminum block heated under heavy driving and tended to expand away from the crankshaft, which increased bearing clearances and dropped oil pressure.

Subtle changes appeared in the later series. In series four, a new grille design was fitted featuring seven vertical bars. The air scoop was flatter. Roger Stowers photo

The solution was found in two increases of sump capacity and the addition of an oil cooler. Thus, first choice for DB4s would be the twenty-one-pint sump with the oil cooler, generally standard at the close of series three production. The oil cooler has often been fitted to earlier cars and would enhance value.

Another solution to low oil pressure is smaller bearing clearances. Factory specifications called for 0.00125 to 0.00175 inch but, according to California Aston Martin Services and similar British authorities, it is possible to go down to as low as 0.0007 inch if the engine is not to be used in a cold climate. Needless to say, tolerances of this minute size require very expert fitting, but when properly done can yield hot oil pressures of over 100 pounds per square inch, substantially higher than the factory-recommended seventy-five pounds. Oil pressure lower than forty-five pounds per square inch hot should not be considered acceptable.

The weep holes on the side of the block should be checked for water leakage which would indicate that the upper O-ring is not sealing properly (see DB MkIII). If oil is found at the weep holes, the lower O-ring is not sealing—but this is very rare since the water is under some pressure from the top and the oil is only being splashed up from the bottom. Also check for gasket leakage at the front end of the head.

Unfortunately, the weep holes are not always a reliable clue for failed upper O-rings. Owners will sometimes put "stop-leak" compounds in the cooling system, which can seal off the weep holes. Such a palliative may work for a long time but if the lower O-ring also perishes, coolant may descend into the sump with serious consequences. Sometimes even sediment may close a weep hole.

Be on the lookout for noisy timing chains, often ignored and rarely adjusted. They should be replaced after 60,000 to 75,000 miles.

In the overhaul of the six-cylinder engines, the valve work is very important. The rather tedious tappet adjustment, which involves the grinding of the valve stems, tempts expedient solutions. Clearances should be loose since a certain amount of settling takes place. Sometimes a very quiet engine after overhaul may have mini-

This 1962 DB4 convertible is much sought after and will bring a price premium of 50 to 100 percent over the saloon. It was introduced at the London Motor Show in 1961 and was available only in the series four and five cars. The top cut was typical of Touring of Milan and the car has an Italianate flavor. Roger Stowers photo

mum or zero clearances after a short time.

The car is heavy and fast. The early single-circuit Dunlop disc brakes were good but can have short life. Unfortunately, Dunlop brake parts are difficult to find. The dual-circuit Girlings are much better with bigger pad areas; the factory can supply these units.

The ten-inch Borg & Beck clutch on the DB4 has much work to do, and heavy pedal pressure does not indicate strength! Wear on the synchromesh cones of the four-speed box may cause them to tip on their saddles, which could block engagement when the box is hot. Richard Williams, a London Aston Martin specialist, suggests a half-hour road test to check gear shifting accuracy.

Corrosion can be a problem, especially on the rear body panel below the bumpers, which was a trap for road dirt. While looking there, also inspect the rear trailing-link mounting points. A more serious rust situation may occur at the forward end of the radius arms; this could affect safety as well as handling. Noise from the front end may also indicate that rubber bushings have perished. Check particularly the rear A-arm where it attaches to the frame. The brake reaction bushing has two aluminum threaded cups which can corrode if exposed to road

The DB4 looked good from any angle. This view shows the late rear lamps. The earlier cars had tall, thin lamps which were also fitted to the

Humber Hawk. John R. Freeman photo from Roger Stowers archives dirt. Excessive movement of the steering wheel may be caused by wear brought on by cracked or broken gaiters on the steering rack. Also check the steering gear mounts.

An unusual corrosion problem may appear in the stud holes caused by fastidious owners washing their engines. The washers beneath the bolts distort and water can collect in the concave faces. Thicker nondistorting washers on the DB5 solved this odd problem.

Heat problems were troublesome, both for the engine and the passengers. The numerous water by-passes through the manifold heaters, the car heater and so on may short-circuit the radiator's best efforts. In some models the underhood louvering was actually reduced or blocked. The heat build-up in the engine compartment is tremendous. In the delightful *Aston Martin in America*, compiler Richard A. Candee has assembled numerous helpful articles on both improving cooling and protecting passengers. Since engine heating directly affects oil pressures on the early cars, buyers should test any DB4 thoroughly to see if problems are present.

Summary and prospects

The DB4 holds numerous opportunities for Aston Martin buyers. It is a very fine car, as evidenced by the continuation of the basic engine design right through the DBS

The dash layout of the DB4 followed the DB Mk III design. This particular car has the Borg Warner automatic transmission which is very rare on the DB4. Louis Klemantaski photo

The DB4 was the first Aston Martin to use the platform frame upon which the body was constructed using square tubular members. This system has continued to the present day. Roger Stowers photo

series. Furthermore, the buyer has the opportunity of selecting a late-series-five car

The later DB4s had substantial interior improvements. The scooped-out rear seats in the DB MkIII style gave way to more conventional seating, admittedly with very thin cushions. The front seats provided improved lateral support. A.C.K. Ware photo

which is virtually identical with the DB5 yet with lower weight. The SS engine models give little away in performance to later models. And those few GT-engined DB4s out there are true giant killers.

Series one DB4s may have the highest potential for vintage racing, certainly on a cost basis. They are around 100 pounds lighter than series twos (worth perhaps 10 hp). Suitably lightened, strengthened and fitted with a GT-specification engine, DB4s are likely the most potent version of the six-cylinder cars.

The opportunity is that the DB4 has been offered over the years at very low prices, often as a result of hard use and low maintenance. The market has thus been dragged down by the presence of many deteriorated examples. There remain available numerous fine DB4s which will provide Aston Martin grand touring or racing at modest prices.

Buyers should carefully identify the car and check for the obvious advantages such

The rear trunk compartment of the DB4 was quite conventional and no longer opened directly into the passenger compartment. The interior trim work was to a high standard. The early type of taillamps fit well with the design. Roger Stowers archives

as the big sump and oil cooler. Even the earliest cars without any of the modifications may well be fine bargains of excellent reliability when driven moderately, which, for an Aston Martin, means performance superior to nearly all other cars. And keep a lookout for the SS-engined models in the earlier series, always worth more. The discovery of a GT engine in a DB4 will enhance value greatly.

Not the least further advantage of the DB4 is that the 3.7 liter engine is not as thirsty as engines in the later cars, an argument for the standard engine. With an over-drive and one of the lower axle ratios, a DB4 can burble along at 60 or 70 mph virtually unstressed and deliver nearly 20 mpg.

Careful buyers will be rewarded with a great car of the highest quality, and owner satisfaction second to none.

Prices for good DB4 saloons are now in the $10,000 to $12,000 range. Exceptional examples may bring more while running but shabby cars can be found at $4,000 to $5,000. Dropheads will be approximately double the price of closed cars in similar condition.

Tadek Marek's new 3670 cc engine was a great success once the oil temperature was reduced. This was accomplished with two increases in sump capacity plus an oil cooler. Reduced bearing clearances also helped. When buying DB4s before the third series, especially check hot oil pressure and look for upgrading modifications. The Aston Martin symbol cast into the valve cover was dropped because it resembled the logo of Volkswagen! Roger Stowers photo

Chapter 15

DB4GT

September 1959-March 1963	
Production: 95 cars total	
coupe	75
Zagato	19
(December 1960-June 1963)	
Bertone	1

History

A short-wheelbase (ninety-three inches) high-performance version of the DB4 was introduced in the fall of 1959. The DB4 engine was fitted with twin ignition from two distributors, three twin-choke Weber carburetors and a 9:1 compression. Brake horsepower was 302 at 6000 rpm. There were minor modifications to some cars, including magnetos, an increased bore to produce 3750 cc and different carburetion layouts.

The GT was offered with five ratios: 2.93, 3.31, 3.54 (standard), 3.77 and 4.09. The Salisbury rear axle was given a Powr-Lok limited slip differential. The four-speed box followed usual specifications but the wide-ratio box was later available. The higher ratios have found recent favor as acceleration is enhanced and clutch loads are reduced.

A lightweight body was originally fitted, which followed the normal styling. The short wheelbase precluded a rear seat (though three cars were so fitted), and a large thirty-six-US-gallon fuel tank was installed with fillers on both sides. Some cars had double seven-US-gallon tanks fitted beneath the fenders. The weight saving was compared to the DB4, second series, was about 185 pounds with an all-up weight of 2,800 pounds.

A DB4GT version bodied by Zagato appeared in 1960, sometimes erroneously referred to as the DB4GTZ. The Zagatos have a 9.7:1 compression ratio producing 314 bhp. The Zagatos have numerous detail modifications from car to car. (See Aston Martin Register, page 152.)

Identification

The short wheelbase, large plated twin fuel fillers and plexiglass-covered headlamps with or without aluminum rims are quick identifiers. The Zagato was very different and followed the typical Zagato body style of the period as found on other Italian makes. Bumper guards were not fitted. The absence of a rear seat was typical.

Chassis numbers: DB4GT/0101/L to DB4GT/0201/L (except 0192 and 0194 to 0198).

Performance and utility

The DB4GT was a powerful performer with 0-60 mph times just over six seconds and 0-100 mph in just over fourteen seconds. The maximum speed was 153 mph

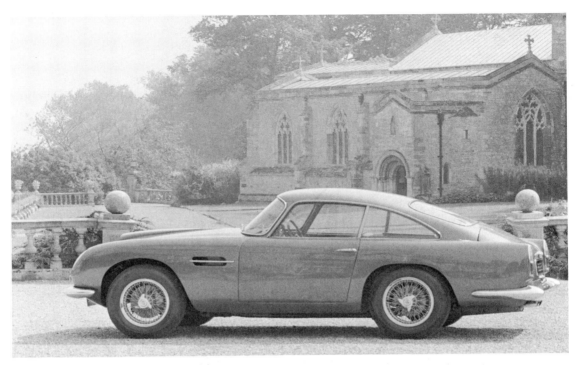

The DB4GT is a very highly regarded car and prices are exceptionally strong. The plexiglass headlight covers may suggest to some the DB5 but a sharp observer can detect the short 93 inch wheelbase and the early DB4 grille. Also this DB4GT has the early, large air scoop. Aston Martin Ltd. photo

using the 3.54 axle. The Girling disc brakes were exceptionally effective. Here was a car that was competition ready.

It was also a car in which everything was a little "closer to the edge." John Wyer felt that the short chassis was not as stable as the normal DB4 chassis. The top piston ring was thinner, the idle was not as smooth and the octane demands were higher. The Zagato had an even higher compression ratio with twelve more horsepower. Competition-minded enthusiasts will welcome these signs of high tune and high performance. Others may find enough performance in the more tractable DB4.

Problem areas

The analysis of the DB4 in Chapter 14 applies to the GT.

The Weber carburetors may occasionally pop back into the air box which, in turn, might contain pooled fuel. To correct this fire hazard, a brass screen was fitted to serve as a flame retarder. Sometimes this screen is incorrectly regarded as an air filter and may be removed or left off during an overhaul.

The lightweight body has thin panels and is easily damaged. Repair of these thin panels is very difficult because distortion and stretching is easy. The Zagato body is especially vulnerable. Careful check should be made for corrosion as well as alignment of doors and windows.

Coachwork

All of the bodies on the GTs are rather special. The nineteen Zagatos are particularly "race handsome" and have found great favor among collectors.

Summary and prospects

The DB4GT is at the very pinnacle of collectibility for Aston Martin enthusiasts, with the Zagato perhaps one of the most sought after sports cars in existence. Prices for the Zagatos are now well into six figures, with £120,000 and up being realized. Owners jealously guard these rare specimens. The DB4GT is now around £25,000

This is DB4GT/0167/R, a works experimental car on a lightweight chassis with an engine to the Zagato specification, producing about 314 bhp. It was road tested by *The Autocar* for its December 18, 1961, issue and achieved a top speed of 152.5 mph. A late grille has been fitted. Roger Stowers archives

The DB4GT Zagato was compact, slightly bulbous and quite unlike any other GT design. Instant recognition has helped boost value.

Jerry Garns photo courtesy of *Motor Trend* and Jerry Rosenstock

The DB4GT Zagato engine was very highly tuned with some 314 bhp available, above the normal GT engine at 302 bhp and far above the advertised 240 bhp in the standard DB4. Zero-to-sixty mph time was at six seconds. Jerry Garns photo courtesy of *Motor Trend* and Jerry Rosenstock

The DB4GT engine, in this instance fitted to a works hybrid, the DB4GT/5/6, built in 1971. Roger Stowers photo

in the UK. The very rapid recent increase in GT prices has tended to force some cars out of competition and into the concours circle. For those lucky owners of a DB4GT, the excitement of driving is hard to beat.

Only 19 of these spectacular DB4GT Zagato coupes were built. Their value is very high, not only by virtue of this rarity but also because of tremendous performance coupled with great beauty. This handsome picture of a 1961 model tells it all. Jerry Garns photo courtesy of *Motor Trend* and Jerry Rosenstock

Chapter 16

DB5

July 1963-September 1965	
Production: 1,021 cars total	
saloon	886
convertible	123
Radford shooting brake	12

History

The DB4 engine was bored out to 96 mm which produced a 3995 cc displacement. On an 8.9:1 compression with three SU HD8 carburetors, 282 bhp was produced at 5500 rpm. In September 1964, the Vantage engine with three Weber carburetors was available, giving 314 bhp at 5750 rpm. A five-speed ZF box was available as an option to the four-speed David Brown fitted with overdrive. The Borg Warner automatic transmission was available on non-Vantage-engined cars and was fitted to about six cars and included a column shift.

Improvements over the similar DB4 series five were an alternator, a handbrake light which also served as a brake-fluid-level warning light, Sundym glass, individual engine gauges though not of the GT type, Girling tandem master brake cylinders with dual brake servos, among other items. A nice option was the Armstrong Selectaride rear shock absorbers.

The convertible and a hardtop option were offered for a £260 premium.

In 1963, a series five DB4 Vantage was modified as a prototype DB5 and given the number DP216/1 with engine number 400/P /4. This car was not only the 1963 Earl's Court show car but in the following year was modified for the James Bond film *Goldfinger*. It has been British registered BMT2-16A and later 6633PP. A second car was built and used in the film which had an opening in the roof and was numbered DB5/1486/R (British registration FMP 7B). The film distribution company then requested that two replicas be built: DB5/2008/R (British registration YRE 186H) and DB5/2017/R (British registration BMT 216). Substantial publicity and added sales resulted from this film. The original 007 Aston Martin and the second car used in the film plus the first replica have been in the USA while the second replica may be in Canada. Prospective buyers of a "James Bond 007" Aston Martin would be well advised to check serial numbers and registration history to determine if the car on offer is, at the least, one of these four cars.

Identification

The plexiglass-covered headlamps have usually set the DB5 apart but it must be remembered that the late-series-five DB4s had the same design. Red warning lights in the door edges and a handbrake warning light were fitted to the DB5. The ZF five-speed gearbox was standard from chassis number 1340, fairly early in production.

Chassis serial numbers: DB5C/1251/R to DB5/2275/L (except 2021, 2094, 2124 and 2125).

Performance and utility

Acceleration figures remained superb. *The Motor* reported 0-60 mph time of 7.1 seconds and a maximum speed of 145 mph. Though the DB5 was 250 pounds heavier than the DB4, the car retained the fine handling characteristics.

When viewed from the rear quarter, the DB5 was very neat. However, rear seating was cramped beneath that smooth, flowing roofline. Roger Stowers archives

Problem areas

A review of the DB4 problems in Chapter 14 will be useful here. The DB5, however, benefited from development. An example would be the five-speed ZF box and the Laycock diaphragm clutch. The front-brake reaction bushing and the upper A-arm bushing were improved. Cooling was also improved. Reliability has been good in these cars.

The DB5 was offered with two types of rear-mounted air-conditioning units. The delivery louvers were located beneath the rear window on the saloon and distorted, or even melted, under intense sunlight.

Coachwork

Harold Radford converted twelve DB5s into handsome estate wagons, which, if for no other reason than their rarity, have found a select market.

The DB5 convertible continued; it is not to be spoken of as a Volante, which was introduced later in the DB6 range. (This is a bit confusing because the first thirty-seven Volantes were built on DB5 chassis with DB6 trim and are called short-chassis Volantes. They were announced and offered for sale at the introduction of the DB6 in

The DB5 in profile was a compact and purposeful car. The rounded front fenders with enclosed lamps set it apart at once from the early DB4s. Many enthusiasts regard the DB5 as the best of the six-cylinder postwar production cars because weight was still modest and power was up. Prices have been healthy and start at about $10,000 for average saloons. Roger Stowers archives

October 1965.) As usual, the convertible DB5 will bring a premium price.

Summary and prospects

Some Aston Martin enthusiasts regard the DB5 as the best of all the postwar production cars. With the shorter wheelbase, ample power from a debugged engine, and still relatively modest weight, the DB5 had everything. Prices have been strong for this series. The top price to date may be £19,000. Usual examples will be found in the $10,000 to $15,000 region. The highest true sale of the DB5 drophead known to me is $65,000. Normal sales of excellent examples will be in the £30,000 area.

Fitted luggage was available for the DB4, DB5 and DB6 and sets occasionally appear on the market. The value of good examples should be in the $1,500 to $2,000 range.

The DB5 convertible was exceptionally neat and will bring a premium price in today's market. An average example can command about $20,000. The DB6 Volante much resembled this car and used the same chassis for the first 37 examples. The DB6 had split bumpers and other differences. Roger Stowers archives

The tube construction of the platform chassis is clearly seen in this factory photo. Sixteen-gauge aluminum was used for paneling. The system is still used. Brian Field photo

A few hardtops were made on the DB5 chassis by the factory. They were of metal, not plastic.
Roger Stowers archives

Harold Radford produced 12 of these exotic shooting brakes on the DB5 chassis and they are much valued. With a 150 mph top speed, Radford claimed that they were the world's fastest dual-purpose vehicle. Harold Radford publicity photo

Chapter 17

DB6

★★
★★★ Volante
★★★★ Shooting brake

October 1965-July 1969	
Production: 1,504 cars total	
saloon	1,321
Radford shooting brake	6
Volante short chassis	37
(October 1965-October 1966)	
Volante	140
(October 1966-July 1969)	

History

The DB6 was announced at the London Motor Show in October 1965 and, though an obvious development of the DB5, was at once seen as bigger and "different." The wheelbase was extended 3¾ inches. The roofline was approximately two inches higher and the rear window did not fade to a point but was upswept. Less noticed was the more raked windshield.

The basic DB5 engine was unchanged but the Vantage power was raised from 314 to 325 bhp. The VC engine had a modified camshaft to enable standard valves to be used.

The typical split bumper of the DB6 is seen on this rare Radford shooting brake. Prices should be high. Roger Stowers archives

Power steering was offered, along with a Powr-Lok limited-slip differential. Air conditioning was also available. The automatic transmission was a no-extra-cost option. Creature comforts were enhanced.

Identification

The rear upswept spoiler, split bumpers and rounded rear windows were instant identifiers of the DB6. An enlarged oil cooler opening appeared below the radiator grille.

The short-chassis Volante is essentially a DB5 but has the DB6 split bumpers, the enlarged oil cooler opening, Triumph tail-lights, a Volante badge on the rear deck and the DB6 interior trim style.

Chassis numbers: DB6/2351/R to DB6/3599/LC, and DB6/4001/R to DB6/4081 (except 4039 and 4061).

Short-chassis Volante numbers: with DBVC/2301/LN to DBVC/2337/R.

Volante numbers: DBVC/3600/R to DBVC/3739/R.

Performance and utility

This mighty car would accelerate to 60

The DB6 Volante was exceptionally handsome and commands strong prices. The squared-off rear fender with spoiler accentuated the length of the open body. Aston Martin photo

The new rear window, no longer pointed, with the rear spoiler instantly identified the DB6. Comfortable four-passenger seating became realistic. The DB6 was a great touring car with very high speeds. Bargains can be found in this model with prices for decent examples at about $10,000. Aston Martin factory photo

from rest in just over six seconds, with a top speed of just under 150 mph. Fuel consumption was increasing and 10 to 12 mpg (US) was reasonable in everyday use, with road mileage perhaps 15 or 16 mpg. The DB6 felt bigger than the DB5, though weight was hardly up. Handling was less agile.

The rear spoiler was a useful design change and increased stability at top speeds.

The DB6 was the first open-bodied Aston Martin to have a power-operated top. It is necessary to have the handbrake on in order to operate the top. The fly-off handbrake fitted to the DB4 and following also mystifies the occasional parking lot attendant.

Problem areas

A review of the DB4 problem areas in Chapter 14 will be useful.

The durable 3995 cc was thoroughly proven and gave little trouble. The Borg & Beck diaphragm clutch has proven to be the best of the series. The DB6 coachwork was slightly less rigid than the DB5. Andrew Whyte notes that the Touring body tooling was abandoned despite the success of the DB4 and DB5 coachwork. The growing complexity of the DB6 with additional servo devices may increase service time.

Though factory body panels are available for the DB6 (and other models beginning with the DB4), the repair of a damaged car is an exacting task. Factory panels only approximate a specification and require expert fitting. Unlike many Italian handmade bodies, the Aston Martin rarely utilizes fillers and metal work must be precise. Repairs to factory standards will be costly.

A possible source of serious trouble is a fuel shortage caused by failure of one of the twin SU fuel pumps, a problem which really becomes important as horsepower and speeds increased in the DB4, DB5 and DB6 series. At high speeds under heavy demand, one pump cannot supply enough fuel and the mixture leans which can produce a burned and holed piston. Unfortunately,

there is no simple way of checking pump operation short of disabling one pump by removing the input wire and then testing.

The window-winding motors on both the DB5 and the DB6 may fail, mainly the result of non-use and condensation getting into the motor contacts. Thus the passenger side usually goes first. Parts are difficult to find. In the DB6 a hand crank is provided in the tool kit in case of failure.

Motor mounts of the DB5 and DB6 are unlike the donut units of the DB4 and were similar to the transmission mounts except that they were used in shear, not in compression. Failure was possible and early replacements were little better. A redesign with improved material has now solved this problem.

Coachwork

There were six Harold Radford shooting brakes built on the DB6 chassis.

Of the 140 regular DB6 Volantes, twenty-nine had Vantage engines and sixty-eight had automatic transmissions. The Volante models bring a substantial premium and should be rated at least three stars.

Summary and prospects

The DB6 remains a thundering touring car of substantial merit. It has not had the particular following of some of the other models, in part because of increased size and a general trend away from the sporting side of the early cars. Even when the DB6s were new, in the late sixties, there was some sales resistance.

The marketing target for the Aston Martin was shifting away from competition-minded enthusiasts to a new affluent clientele. In recognition of this shift, prices for both the Vantage and the automatic versions were the same, removing any stigma which might have been attached to shiftless motoring. Today these cars can be found at very modest prices, yet a DB6 automatic, admittedly with a factory rebuild, recently brought £20,000. More usual prices will be in the $10,000 region. The Volante will not be found in the bargain basement, however, and prices for fine examples have gone as high as $40,000.

The design of the Radford shooting brake managed to incorporate the rear spoiler in a neat way. Not many motorists will ever see this view, as only six were built. Roger Stowers archives

Chapter 18

DB6 Mk2

★★
★★★ Volante

July 1969-November 1970
Production: 278 cars total
   saloon   240
   Volante   38

History

Time was running out for the DB6, still being produced despite the presence of the DBS since October 1967. A final refinement was made in the DB6 Mk2 series. Engine specifications were virtually unchanged, though one new option available was the AE Brico fuel-injection system which was fitted to forty-six cars. The Vantage engine option was continued. Power steering was standard. A bigger clutch was fitted. Automatic transmission and limited-slip differential were no-cost options. Tire size was now 8.15x15, which necessitated opening and flaring the wheel arches.

Of the thirty-eight Volantes built, twenty-one had automatic transmission and nine had the five-speed box with the Vantage engine.

Identification

The DB6 Mk2 series is easily spotted by the flares on the wheel arches, the larger hubs with three-eared hub nuts flattened closer to the spokes and the wider six-inch rims.

Chassis numbers: DB6Mk2/41001/R to DB6Mk2/4345/R.

Volante chassis numbers: DB6Mk2VC/3751/R to DB6Mk2VC/3788/L.

Performance and utility

The wider, six-inch rims with 8.15×15 tires gave more road contact and better handling and cornering.

Problem areas

A review of the basic DB4 engine problems in Chapter 14 may be useful.

The AE Brico fuel-injection system was installed before development was completed and it gave much trouble. Very few cars can still be so fitted, and the factory service department converted most of the injection systems to Weber carburetors. It is a pity that the Brico system was not perfected because when it was right it gave superior performance to the Vantage engine and superior economy to the basic SU carburetors. The Mk2 has the final refinement and accompanying reliability of the whole series.

Coachwork

The Volante convertible continued as the only option to the saloon and found good demand. The price rose, until in 1970 it was $13,053 (£4,662), up from $11,578 (£4,135) in 1965. This was nothing com-

The AE Brico electronic fuel-injection system on the DB6 Mk2 had the difficult-to-work-on electronic "black box," which was all too often unreliable. Most enthusiasts prefer carburetors. Aston Martin Lagonda Ltd. photo

The DB Mk2 engine with carburetors is now preferred over the injection system. Reliability is excellent and performance gives little away to the more complex AE Brico system. P.H.U. Blume photo

The final frontal appearance of the DB6 Mk2 still echoes that of the DB MkIII. It is a timeless and pleasing design. P.H.U. Blume photo

pared with what came in 1978 when the next Volante model was offered at £28,944 or approximately $69,000.

Summary and prospects

This last of the old line going back to the DB4 is undoubtedly a desirable collectible, and some would argue that the Mk2 is a pinnacle of perfection. Prices have occasionally reached the $15,000 to $20,000 area for fine examples. The Volante has proven to be a most attractive model with accompanying high prices, up to $30,000 and more.

The new wheel arches of the Mk2 worked well with the smooth DB6 line. This final version of the DB4 Touring-designed body had excellent balance and some regard it as the best of the line. Prices have been in the $15,000 to $20,000 area. Roger Stowers archives

Chapter 19

DBS ★

October 1967-May 1972
Production: 787 cars total

History

The DBS was first shown on September 25, 1967. It was styled by William Towns, who had joined Aston Martin in 1966. Touring in Milan had prepared two lightweight prototypes (the DBSC) for a "next generation" replacement for the DB6 which were brought to England and tested. These two were pretty cars, not unlike the Lamborghini 400. Towns' drawings were much different, however, with sharp body edgings and an upright grille. The new car was also big, much wider than either of the two Touring prototypes, and (at 3,500 pounds) some 200 pounds heavier than the DB6 Mk2. The wheelbase was one inch longer and the platform chassis was 4½ inches wider. The body was six inches wider but 1½ inches shorter than the DB6, which gave the car a powerful, compact appearance. Both Andrew Whyte and Wilson McComb reported that David Brown wanted the car narrower, but the body jigs were already in place.

The car was prepared for Tadek Marek's new V8 engine which was not ready. Thus the mechanical specification was similar to that of the DB6. The standard engine produced 282 bhp; the Vantage version was listed at 325 bhp. However, a de Dion rear axle was fitted with coil springs. The ratios were much higher, 3.54:1 with the Borg Warner automatic and 3.73:1 with the five-speed ZF transmission, though in fifth gear the ZF final ratio was 3.11:1.

Identification

The four quartz iodine lamps set in the new semi-razor-edged body of massive proportion quickly identify the new DBS. Louvers behind the rear window for interior exhausting were used until the end of 1969, followed by a louver ahead of the trunk lid. Early models had a wood-faced instrument panel.

Normal engines have the suffix S; Vantage engines will have the suffix SVC (i.e., 400/—/SVC).

Chassis numbers: DBS/5001/R to DBS/-5829/RC (but thirty-nine numbers were not used).

Performance and utility

Top speed fell to about 140 mph, the penalty of added weight and increased frontal area. Such speed would hardly be considered inadequate especially when the 0-60 time averaged about eight seconds, but the DB6 could manage about 150 mph with 0-60 in 6.5 seconds. Expectations about Aston Martin standards were very high.

Interior room was much enhanced. Air conditioning, noted by an AC in the chassis number, was increasingly fitted but was only marginally effective because of the increased glass area. General Motors AC window-winding motors were fitted and have proven reliable. Fuel consumption could be as low as 10 mpg (US) though light-footed cruising with the five-speed box might bring it up to 18 mpg.

Problem areas

The AE Brico fuel-injection system was offered on this car and has not proven reliable. The front wishbone is anchored to the chassis platform by a rubber-covered ball in an aluminum casting, which has been known to pull out under severe use. Check for wear and corrosion. The new bodies had some problems with leaking and corrosion—the usual areas should be checked around sills and wheel spatter areas. The door-stop linkages were weak, loaded by a heavy door and trim weighing ten pounds.

Electrical problems are not uncommon in the DBS, partly the result of new model complexity.

Emissions suppression was becoming a general problem for companies desiring to sell in the US market. Aston Martin's US

A light color emphasized the bulk of the new DBS. The greater width of the car was especially noticeable. Surface development at the rear was well controlled. British prices for these cars have been low, around £5,000. Roger Stowers archives

export model was fitted with Stromberg carburetors which have proven troublesome.

Coachwork

According to the Aston Martin Register, all of the DBSs were saloons with the exception of one shooting brake conversion by FLM Panelcraft.

Summary and prospects

The six-cylinder engine in the new DBS body makes an attractive proposition for the buyer interested in a contemporary-looking Aston Martin with economical maintenance. The proven durability of the old engine makes it a desirable used car. Performance in the over-100 mph region, the place where the V8 engine really shines, may not be a major consideration to some users, although Aston Martin enthusiasts are fond of calling this model sluggish, despite a top speed of 140 mph! However, slow sales of the DBS, when new, have tended to warp the subsequent market to the advantage of today's buyers. When compared to the DB6 Mk2, the DBS seems bigger, slower and less refined. Paul Chudecki rightly calls this model "the last and most underrated of the David Brown, Aston Martin sixes."

The interior of the DBS was in the best British tradition, with rich leather and carpeting and a full instrument array. The heavy, ten-pound door trim is clearly visible in this photo. Aston Martin Lagonda Ltd. photo

Prices have reached nadir in this model. The car was slower and much larger than the DB6 and seemed to lose sporting characteristics. Many enthusiasts were disappointed when the DBS first appeared. As a new model, the car had early problems and development and refinement were needed. The Vantage engine helped performance but US models were not so equipped. In addition, the export models often had automatic transmissions and were even more sluggish.

UK prices are in the £5,00 area and US prices are usually below $10,000. Automatics will bring even less.

On the other hand, the two DBSC prototypes by Touring may well be worth £45,000, according to one expert.

On September 13, 1968, the factory crash-tested the new DBS at 30 mph into a concrete block. It met both the 1968 and 1970 US requirements. Aston Martin Lagonda Ltd. photo

This 1971 DBS had the new body, though mechanicals resembled the DB6 Mk2. The quad headlamps did not last beyond the DBSV8. Prices for these cars are low and they may be the best bargain of all Aston Martins. Aston Martin Lagonda Ltd. photo

Chapter 20

DBSV8

April 1970-May 1972
Production: 399 cars total

History

The 5340 cc V8 engine entered production in 1969. The ninety-degree twin cam engine was designed by Tadek Marek and was race tested with various displacements. Following Le Mans in 1967 the engine was substantially modified which delayed introduction and is the reason that the DBS appeared with the old six-cylinder engine.

At 9:1 compression, the V8 produced about 375 bhp. Engines that met US emissions standards had the suffix EE. Bosch

Looking very much like the DBS, the DBSV8 made its debut in the spring of 1970. The major exterior difference was the aluminum wheels which gave a "tough" appearance to the car. This car was exceptionally fast with 0-60 mph times under six seconds, and top speeds near 170 mph. Low prices make this car the performance bargain of all time. Aston Martin Lagonda Ltd. photo

fuel injection was used. A Chrysler three-speed automatic was offered along with the ZF five-speed box. The car weighed 3,800 pounds.

Production changes included a leather-covered steering wheel, a glovebox mounted on top of the transmission and lower rear axle ratios. (A full treatment of the development of this engine may be found in Wilson McComb's fine book, *Aston Martin V8s*.)

Identification

Fifteen-inch aluminum wheels with broad seven-inch rims replaced the wire wheels of the DBS. In other external respects, the DBSV8 was similar to the DBS. This was the last series with four headlamps.

Chassis numbers: DBSV8/10001/R to DBSV8/10405/RCA.

Performance and utility

The DBSV8 was an astounding performer with 0-60 times of under six seconds and a top speed of 160 mph. This was amazing because of the car's weight. Huge Girling ventilated disc brakes complemented the acceleration. No production car could touch these maximum speeds. Fuel economy was poor, but until 1974, when gasoline prices began to climb, this was hardly a consideration.

Problem areas

The long gestation period of the V8 engine may have been the reason this unit has earned such an enviable reputation. Its long-wearing qualities, ability to sustain tune under hard usage and the very high mileages without rebuild have made the V8 engine virtually invisible when considering the buying of a car. The engines rarely give trouble.

Nevertheless, inspection should be made of the weep holes to check O-ring sealing at the base of the cylinder liners, one of the features Marek continued from the six-cylinder engine. There is a chance of valve-guide wear on early units but the problem is not serious.

The Bosch fuel-injection system was not entirely satisfactory, a problem of com-

This 1972 DBSV8 had air conditioning as standard equipment. Production ended in May 1972. Late cars had a leather-covered steering wheel, glovebox in the center console and pockets in the back of the front seats. Rear seating was improved. Aston Martin Ltd. photo

plexity and improper servicing. Starting when hot was erratic because of vaporization of fuel. This was solved by fitting a cold-starting enrichment overrider activated by the pushing of a dash-mounted button marked S. The additional raw fuel was enough to get started.

A more obscure starting problem was caused by the splitting of a small plastic connecting tube inside the aluminum balance manifold, impossible to diagnose without dismantling the manifold!

The Selectaride shock absorbers were last fitted to the DBSV8 and have given trouble. Delicate adjustment is required and the solenoids have not proven to be stable.

Spark plugs have a short life because of increased emission controls. Platinum plug replacements have helped.

A peculiar problem was the habit of the factory fitting some of the many solenoids upside down, which made them function as water traps and was followed by early failure. This may have been a symptom of a more general decline of quality control that plagued the DBSV8. The company was in financial trouble which resulted in a lowering of worker morale. Quality suffered at the very time when the best efforts were needed to save the marque. US export models were reputedly given more careful scrutiny.

The car was heavy and the front suspension was working at the design limits. Wear was rapid and a thorough inspection of the ball joints and mounting is recommended.

Coachwork
The saloon was the only body offered on the DBSV8.

Summary and prospects
The DBSV8 was not available in the United States until late in 1971, but the price of meeting the ever-more-stringent standards was reduced power. Wilson McComb believes that the delay in introducing the V8 in the US was crucial for the fortunes of the company. Furthermore, all US models had automatic transmission, necessary to meet emissions requirements. A handful of DBSV8s have the ZF five-speed box, either by conversion or by private importing of UK models. The automatic was strong but again reminded enthusiasts of the break in traditions. Only about thirty-seven DBSV8s were sold new in the US.

The blinding speed of the first fuel-injected V8 was not equaled in the models that immediately followed, as smog controls reduced power. Thus, performance enthusiasts will seek out the early DBSV8s. Following the fuel shortages of the seventies, these cars were often knocked down to low prices and may still be found at low prices, in the $5,000 to $10,000 region with outstanding examples as high as $15,000. This car could be the performance bargain of the decade.

This was the last David Brown Aston Martin and it was a powerful conclusion to a great era.

The DBSV8 engine of 5340 cc was a tremendous engine which has been steadily developed into one of the most reliable, high-output engines of all time. This early version has the Bosch fuel injection, a mechanical system better than the Brico electronic injection yet replaced in 1973 by Weber carburetors. Aston Martin Ltd. photo

Chapter 21

AM Vantage ★

| May 1972-July 1973 |
| Production: 70 cars total |

History

The AM Vantage was a continuation of the DBS series under the new ownership of Company Developments Ltd. The Aston Martin Register editors point out that the term "Vantage" had heretofore been used with tuned production versions and its use as a model designation is novel.

The front end changes recalled the earlier traditional Aston Martin shape and were altogether pleasing. The quad headlamps were dispensed with in favor of two seven-inch quartz iodine lamps. Mechanical specifications were similar to the DBS.

Identification

The modified two-headlamp DBS body shape with a six-cylinder engine is distinctive.

The chassis numbers omitted all reference to "DB" as Sir David Brown departed from the scene though, for a short time, the old badge stock continued to be fitted.

Chassis numbers: AM/6001/R to AM/-6070/R.

Performance and utility

The great six-cylinder Tadek Marek engine was in its final form and, like all en-gines, long production life even without redesign brings better quality. The running costs of the AM Vantage should be favorable when compared to the V8.

Performance is similar to the DBS: a top of around 140 and a 0-60 time of about eight seconds.

Problem areas

The running gear was understressed by the six-cylinder engine, and little trouble may be expected. The engine was thoroughly proven and again had few faults.

Coachwork

The AM Vantage was produced only in saloon form.

Summary and prospects

The rarity of this model plus the fact that it was not sold in the United States suggests a narrow market. The revised grille, mechanical refinement, lower operating costs and superb detailing give to this last six-cylinder Aston Martin a charm which discerning collectors will appreciate. Performance is tremendous; it suffers only by comparison to the V8. In the longest perspective, the AM Vantage may turn out to be one of the most usable and desirable of the recent Aston Martins. Prices have been soft, again because of the inevitable comparison made to the V8-engined models.

The Aston Martin Vantage was a continuation of the six-cylinder DBS under the new ownership after David Brown, Company Developments Ltd. Use of the term "Vantage" was contrary to Aston Martin practice which had always reserved the term for tuned versions of standard cars. The new front-end design was similar to the V8 models. Only 70 were built and none were sold in the US. Prices will be low. Aston Martin Ltd. photo

Chapter 22

AMV8

★ Series 2
★★ Series 3
★★★ Series 4
★★★★ Volante

April 1972-present
Production: approximately 2,124 cars total
V8 series 2	286
(April 1972-July 1973)	
V8 series 3	973
(August 1973-September 1978;	
not built in 1975)	
V8 series 4	299
(October 1978 through	
December 31, 1985)	
V8 Volante	approximately 350
(June 1978 to present)	
V8 Vantage	approximately 215
(see Chapter 23)	

History

The David Brown Corporation sold out to Company Developments Ltd. in January 1972. Production continued until December 31, 1974, at which time the company went into receivership. Production resumed in the spring of 1976 under the new ownership of Peter Sprague, George Minden, Alan Curtis and Denis Flather as Aston Martin Lagonda 1975 Ltd. (1975 was dropped in 1980). The ownership transferred in 1981 to C. H. Industrials and Pace Petroleum. The firm is now managed by Victor Gauntlett.

The basic design has been maintained during this turbulent period but very many improvements and innovations have taken place, making the current product a very different car from the original DBSV8. Aston Martin's astonishing powers of recovery stem in large measure from the tremendous esteem in which enthusiasts hold the firm throughout the world. The car is too good to die and remains one of those rare marques whose quality has been maintained without compromise throughout its entire history.

Identification

The editors of the Aston Martin Owners Club Register—Jane Archer, Tony Byles, Inman Hunter and Alan Archer—have developed a series system for analyzing the V8s, which deserves expanded use. It is summarized from the register as follows:

Series 1. The DBSV8 (detailed in Chapter 20). These were the fuel-injected four-headlight models made during the closing years of the David Brown ownership of the company.

Series 2. The AMV8 was no longer built by David Brown, although the first nineteen cars, through V8/10519/RCA, still had the David Brown badge. Two seven-inch quartz iodine lights replaced the quad headlamps. The grille was entirely new, no longer sweeping across the whole front of the car but tailored between the headlamps in an outline more like the earlier DB six-cylinder series. The spare tire was stowed flat for enlarged luggage space. Transistorized ignition was fitted. The cam covers read

"Aston Martin Lagonda."

Series 3. Four twin-choke Weber carburetors replaced the Bosch fuel-injection system. The bulge on top of the hood was raised and extended all the way back to the rear edge. The front seats were redesigned and the door locks were electrically controlled. The fuses may be found in the glovebox.

Series 4. The air scoop on the front of the hood bulge was deleted. The rear of the car by the taillights was smoothed and a spoiler was added. Wood trim was applied on the dash and leather was used in the headlining. Air conditioning was improved. Later changes included interior switching for the trunk and gas caps, and optional cruise control. Numerous engine refinements were also introduced which improved fuel economy. An important improvement was the stainless steel exhaust system. Geometry settings for the front suspension were changed. In recognition of improved reliability, service intervals were extended to 5,000 miles.

The cars of this series were essentially like those being produced today. Another useful clue in recognizing these cars is the wood fillets which are used on the doors.

A summary of serial numbers may be useful.

Series 1: DBSV8/10001/R to DBSV8/-10405/RCA. Special suffixes: C=coolair, AC=air conditioning, after 1971 A=acrylic paint.

Series 2: V8/10501/RCA to V8/10789.

Series 3: V8/11001/R to V8/12000; V8/-12010 to V8/12031/RCAV (12001 to 12009

The new Aston Martin was announced on April 24, 1972, with a revised front end. The outline of the grille was more like the DB6, and the two headlamps also picked up earlier styling themes. Mechanical changes were minor. Aston Martin Lagonda Ltd. photo

were Logondas). Special suffixes: EE=Japanese emissions standards, LFM (lead-free manual)=US emission standards, S=special tune. V on engine number=Vantage engine (see Chapter 23).

Series 4: V8SOR/12032 forward. C=convertible (V8COR 15001 and up), V (prefix)= Vantage (V8VOR), V (suffix) on engine number=Vantage (possible on standard series cars—see Chapter 23).

Performance and utility

The AMV8 in all of the series has maintained a reputation for unbeatable performance. Zero-to-sixty times have hovered around six seconds, with maximum speeds in the 150 to 160 mph range. The times are even better with the Vantage engine (detailed in Chapter 23).

The US models suffer in comparison because horsepower is reduced by lower compression and by emissions equipment. A higher-ratio differential gear is fitted to enhance acceleration, and top speed of US models is about 130 mph.

The third series of Aston Martins began in August 1973. The Bosch fuel injection was dropped in favor of four Weber carburetors, which necessitated a raised bulge in the hood, clearly emphasized in this frontal view. The company went into receivership at the end of 1974; production stopped but was resumed in the spring of 1976 under new ownership with essentially the same car. Pictured here is one of the 1976 models. Aston Martin Lagonda Ltd. photo

Coachwork

The V8 Volante convertible was announced in June 1978 and had walnut interior trim. Weight was up 150 pounds over the saloon. Early production was exclusively for the US. The price of the Volante was about £6,000 higher than the corresponding saloon, a difference that has gradually increased to about £8,000. In the used market, the Volante commands very much higher prices.

Problem areas

When production was resumed in 1976, the new management undertook a major review of the car with four objectives: one, to improve quality control in manufacture; two, to redesign any component which had a poor service history; three, to redesign any component which could refine or improve performance; four, to enhance the amenities and ambiance of the car to the highest possible levels. A partial listing of the results appears above.

Armstrong shock absorbers replaced the Selectaride units and were, in turn, replaced by Konis. It should be noted that improvements were introduced when ready and

The revived company of 1975 was able to begin production for 1976 with the previous 1973 third-series car, but at the same time Alan Curtis and his team were working on a much revised AMV8. The prototype of the new car was called Oscar India (probably meaning October 1, 1978), and defined the fourth series which began in October 1978. The new rear fenderline was evident, along with the absence of the scoop at the front of the hood bulge. Cars after this date had many improvements. Values go up sharply in this fourth series. Aston Martin Lagonda Ltd. photo

were not withheld to fit a series change. For example, when the Koni shock absorbers were first fitted, some cars were given Armstrong shocks at the front and Konis at the rear until old inventory was exhausted. With many changes taking place, cars with later chassis numbers will be more desirable, especially those after late 1977. Cars built after this time should be more reliable.

The automatic remote door locks have given trouble on some of the early cars. This may often be cured by simply increasing the size of the wire feeding the solenoids.

Occasional fires occurred in the engine compartments of early cars, cured by fitting a brass wire screen across the air intake opening of the carburetor box to prevent flame blow-back. Do not mistake this screen for an air filter.

The refinement of the AMV8 is obvious in this frontal view. Though this picture is dated 1979, the basic design has remained unchanged since 1978. Prices rose very steeply after 1978, the result of serious cost studies along with rising labor rates. Improvements have been steady and buyers in this market may yet find bargains in the early fourth-series production which gives little away to current models. Aston Martin Lagonda Ltd. photo

Summary and prospects

Below is a year-by-year summary of the factory prices of the basic Aston Martin V8 saloon without tax.

Year	Price	Year	Price
1969	£5,281	1977	£14,187
1970	£5,744	1978	£19,657
1971	£6,110	1979	£23,076
1972	£7,405	1980	£27,691
1973	£8,050	1981	£30,501
1974	£9,700	1982	£32,106
1975	£10,910	1983	£34,112
1976	£13,333		

The situation becomes more dramatic by comparing US prices for recent saloon models:

Year	Model	Price
1962	DB4	$10,000
1964	DB5	$12,995
1966	DB6	$15,495
1970	DBSV8	$20,000 (approx.)
1977	AMV8	$33,950
1980	AMV8 Volante	$79,650 (auto.)
		$81,500 (5-speed)
1983	AMV8	$96,000

The fob price rose sharply after 1977, doubling in just four years. The US price tripled in the seven years after 1977. To be sure, there has been some stability in recent new car prices in the US caused in part by the substantial devaluation of the pound sterling. The following is a comparison of US prices.

Model	1985	1983 and 1984
AMV8 saloon	$100,000	$96,000
Vantage	$110,000	
Volante	$125,000	$115,000
Lagonda	$150,000	$150,000

A used market for the V8 thus must reflect this extraordinary price increase. Buyers prepared to pay $100,000 for a new Aston Martin are not likely to be lured by an $80,000 used car. On the other hand, the relative continuity of the AMV8 makes possible prestige ownership of a used car very much like that of current production models for a substantially lower price. This has enhanced used-car prices.

The same principle has worked for Rolls-Royce for many years and has helped sustain values. Aston Martin buyers of new V8s prior to 1977 may now have the pleasant surprise of driving depreciation-free automobiles. Even those who bought prior to

After a 7½ year absence, Aston Martin re-entered the convertible market in June 1978 with the new Volante built on the AMV8 platform chassis. Demand was immediate and not surprising in light of the prices for the used, older DB5 and DB6 convertibles. The opening price was £28,944, quite a premium when compared to £19,657 for the saloon. That differential seems to have remained in the used market. This picture is of the first Volante and is dated June 4, 1978. Aston Martin Ltd. photo

1980, especially the Volante owners, are in an enviable position.

There is thus the interesting situation in the British market that the DBSV8 and AMV8 saloons of the seventies now have asking prices approximating those of their new prices, assuming excellent condition. Volante asking prices are less predictable but always strong. For example, a new Volante that sold in June 1984 for £53,000 was repurchased by the factory a year later for £51,250, surely modest depreciation by any standard.

It will be noticed that the British price in sterling is substantially lower than the American price in dollars, which raises the possibility of importing a Continental left-hand-drive model and converting to federal DOT standards. The problems are formidable. US gasoline is now about four octane points lower than UK top ratings.

The first conversion is to install low-compression pistons, which requires an engine dismantling. A catalytic converter is then fitted, along with carbon canisters. The carburetors must be encased to protect against fuel evaporation. Crush bars must be installed in the doors. Fitting of the higher-ratio US-specification differential would be useful. After these modifications are made, the car must be retuned and calibrated and then put through the usual testing procedures, a critical matter on extreme-performance engines.

It is often forgotten that the research and development costs for US-specification models must be amortized by US sales, which were approximately seventy-five units in 1985. Furthermore, US product requirements amount to some $5,000 per car, entirely apart from smog controls. Aston Martin Lagonda Ltd. must take into account

Even with the top up, the Volante is very handsome. Its introduction, when convertibles were being phased out by US domestic makers, was fortuitous product planning and helped focus attention on this mighty car. Especially in profile, it is easy to see why the Volante has become a standout. Every luxury was provided, including polished burl walnut trim. This car presently lists for $125,000 in the US and demand is brisk. Aston Martin Ltd. photo

all of these added costs when attempting to price and market cars in the US. The perceived price differential is substantially reduced when these factors are considered; in fact, it disappears at a certain dollar-sterling exchange rate.

About 1978, in the series 4 production, the quality level of the Aston Martins was higher, the result of intensive effort beginning in 1975. Buyers of V8 models in the series 4 have reported a very satisfactory level of reliability.

The AMV8 series remains at the very peak of the high-performance luxury market. Consistent development has produced a car of marvelous refinement and dependability. The limited production of such a high-quality hand-built car ensures long-range collectibility and value. Buyers of these cars may also take comfort in strong factory service support. In particular, the Volante, always a premium item, has proven to be an especially sound investment since 1978.

The prototype Volante weighed about 4,000 pounds. Vantage engines were not specified for the Volante, but the power of the standard engine was more than enough to attain very high speeds in the 140 to 150 mph region. The used market for these cars is very strong and early-version buyers have been rewarded with nearly depreciation-free ownership, thanks in part to steep price increases. Aston Martin Ltd. photo

Chapter 23

AMV8 Vantage ★★★★

May 1977-present (not sold in the US)
Production: approximately 215 cars total
V8 series 3	43
V8 series 4	172

(through December 31, 1985, and including "cosmetic" Vantages for the USA)

History

Though the AMV8 Vantage is a model variation of the AMV8 series, the Aston Martin Register editors have chosen to present this car as a separate section, a useful convention which is followed here.

Throughout the life of the Aston Martin, the term "Vantage" has been used to designate a tuned version of the standard production engine (apart from the AM Vantage series). In the case of the V8 engine, the tuning meant a general improvement of breathing, including larger valves, a new camshaft with more overlap, bigger twin-choke Weber 48 IDF2/100 carburetors and new intake manifolds. Brake horsepower was around 408.

Chassis changes included stiffening of the suspension, Koni shocks and a larger antiroll bar.

Identification

The AMV8 Vantage has a front spoiler extending very low and a rear spoiler neatly faired into the body. The radiator grille is blanked off. There is no undertray on the Vantage, as air must be drawn up. Cibie driving lamps are fitted. The standard tires are Pirelli P7 275/55 UR15s.

The various external specifications may not always indicate a Vantage model. This is because the factory, unable to export Vantages to the US on account of emission controls, constructs "cosmetic" Vantages with normal engines, according to Michael Bowler, engineering director. Thus the chance of a true Vantage engine appearing in any Aston Martin V8 in the US market is very remote, no matter what the external appearance may be. Buyers should be wary of sellers' claims to the contrary.

On the other hand, some of these US cosmetic Vantages have been given a genuine upgrade to Vantage engine specifications. The larger Weber carburetors will be one clue but much of the work is internal. Owners who have gone to the expense of this conversion will probably be eager to prove their claim to prospective buyers.

Engine serial numbers should be checked. Look for a final V.

Series 1: Chassis, V8/11563/RCAV and up. Engine, V/540/1563/V and up. (Here the final V indicates Vantage on both serial and engine numbers.)

Series 2: Chassis, V8VOR/12040 and up.

Engine, V/540/2040/V and up. (Here only the engine number has the final V.)

Performance and utility

The AMV8 Vantage lays claim to being the world's most extraordinary high-performance automobile. Zero-to-sixty times are as low as 5.2 seconds with a top speed approaching 180 mph. The phenomenal thing is that this car weighs 3,800 pounds and it is not turbocharged. Manual-transmission cars are fitted with the 3.33:1. A 2.88:1 ratio is used with the automatic transmission.

The great Vantage engine has no redline and is safe to 7000 rpm, though at the recommended 6250 rpm the top gear is no less than 130 mph with normal axle ratio. Road stability is without fault.

The great thing about the Vantage is that all of this blinding performance is done in the traditional manner, with refinement and remarkably low noise levels. The absence of a turbocharger means that the power flow is consistent without any narrowing of the useful rev range. The stopping power is 1.2 g, from huge disc brakes. The cornering power is about 0.9 g. Handling is predictable. This great car offers all of the refinements of the grand tourer,

yet with a general performance level that is superior to all other highly tuned and often nervous sports cars available.

Problem areas

The Vantage appeared during the quality control effort and, because of its nature as a super performance car, received the closest attention. It was thus spared from the problems of the early seventies. Reliability should be excellent.

The extraordinary torque and power of

The Oscar India prototype of the Vantage in October 1978 became the Series 2. The very low front spoiler and blanked-off radiator were readily evident. The hood scoop was smoothly faired in. Aston Martin Lagonda Ltd. photo

The early first-series Vantage had the rear spoiler "added on" and the seam showed. Both the radiator and the air scoop were blanked off.

This car did 0-60 mph in 5.3 seconds. Prices for any Vantage AMV8 will be high. Aston Martin Lagonda Ltd. photo

the Vantage engine puts maximum stress on the driveline components. The Chrysler Torqueflite transmission has proven to be tough and durable. However, there have been a few failures of the differential under extreme use.

Coachwork

The AMV8 Vantage is offered only in saloon form. In March 1986 the Zagato-bodied special was offered at a price of £87,000. Performance reached incredible levels with a 0-60 mph time of 4.8 seconds. Production was scheduled at two per month, and about fifty units were presold. If past Zagato-bodied Aston Martins are any guide, this new version should have exceptional future market prospects.

Summary and prospects

There seems every likelihood that the AMV8 Vantage is going to go down in history as one of the all-time high-performance cars, similar in reputation to the Bentley R type Continental. Enthusiasts who appreciate such performance in a car that can be driven casually for both utility and general pleasure could do no better.

The price has risen dramatically from 1977, which has helped to sustain values for the Vantage.

Year	Price	Year	Price
1977	£17,093	1981	£32,106
1978	£22,221	1982	£34,113
1979	£26,086	1983	£38,126
1980	£29,698	1985	£45,748

Lucky buyers of early Vantages have seen little diminution of the value of their investments. This trend may continue but at a slower rate. The new Zagato of 1986 will likely have a superior long-range market position.

This particular Vantage was road tested by *Motor* on April 25, 1981, and produced a 0-60 time of 5.2 seconds, since improved to 5.1 seconds. The big Pirelli P7 tires may be a factor in getting all that power to the ground. Such acceleration in a car weighing 3,800 pounds can only be described as awesome. Aston Martin Lagonda Ltd. photo

The instrument panel of the Vantage was for serious motoring. The automatic transmission was fitted to a few cars such as this one. Enthusiasts preferred the five-speed box; yet, with virtually unlimited power, an automatic hardly penalized performance and produced very speedy, consistently smooth and anxiety-free shifting—a useful combination of assets. Automatics have greatly broadened the market for the company, especially in the AMV8 series. Aston Martin Lagonda Ltd. photo

The blanked-off hood scoop, covered radiator opening and add-on rear spoiler are clearly seen on this Series 1 Vantage. This picture is dated December 2, 1977. Aston Martin Lagonda Ltd. photo

Renewing a long-standing relationship between Aston Martin and the Zagato coachworks in Italy, the V8 Zagato announced in early 1986 is a masterpiece. The first production run was sold out instantly. Certainly, the likeness is there when you compare it to the DB4GT Zagato. Roger Stowers photos

Chapter 24

Specials, one-offs and prototypes

From 1948 until 1963, the factory had a vigorous competition program which was finally terminated because the design requirements of winning cars became increasingly unrelated to production models. Factory competition cars were treated in the appropriate chapters but there were other works prototypes and specials which usually had serial numbers beginning with DP.

In more recent times, private builders have produced numerous prototypes and specials using Aston Martin components and often built around the great Aston Martin V8 engine. These cars may not be

DP212, here shown alongside DBR1/2, was the team car at Le Mans in 1962 and was in second place in the sixth hour when a piston was holed.

The engine was a DB4GT unit of 3996 cc displacement which gave a maximum of 345 bhp at 6000 rpm. Roger Stowers photo

Aston Martins in that they were not "conceived, built, assembled and sold" by the factory. Others, however, are highly modified factory production cars. Most of these cars are in private hands but since all are unique, an estimate of market value is difficult. Prospective buyers should consult *The Aston Martin Register* to determine present ownership and possible availability.

The following pictures represent some of these specials and prototypes, both by the factory and by private builders.

DP212 has been driven often by Mike Salmon, here shown giving owner John Downe the wheel for a tour d'honneur following another victory. Roger Stowers photo

DP214 (DB4GT/0194/R) first appeared at Le Mans in 1963 and retired after 1,965 km. With Weber carburetors, the bhp was 310. Though specifications began with the DB4GT, there were many major modifications. The car has been much raced both by the works and privately, and has a fine record. Roger Stowers photo

DP215, another experimental prototype, appeared in June 1963 and was the last factory team car. It retired at Le Mans after 403 km. A dry-sump 3996 cc engine produced 345 bhp with Weber carburetors. The car was badly damaged on the M1 in 1966 but was given a new spare body. Roger Stowers photo

This is one of the two prototypes for the DBS built by Touring, 266/2/L. They were subsequently called the DBSC, since they had only two seats and were substantially smaller than the DBS. 266/2/L was shown at Earl's Court in 1966. Roger Stowers photo

Here is a real oddity, one of the two Ogle-built DBSV8 cars. They were used by Sotheby/Embassy as public relations cars. Shown is DB-SV8/10381/RC. The second special, DBS-V8/10581/RCA, was a great deal more civilized. Roger Stowers photo

Keith Martin stands proudly beside the Bulldog, V8TLSM, designed by a team under his direction. The striking car was introduced on April 15, 1980. The gull-wing doors were designed by Bill Towns and are power operated. Roger Stowers photo

The extraordinary headlamp display was re-vealed by a hinged panel, the lowering of which must have introduced substantial drag. Roger Stowers photo

The dramatic profile of the Bulldog hints at the mid-chassis mounting of the twin-turbo V8, reputed to have 60 percent more power than the Vantage engine. Roger Stowers photo

The Bulldog was a two-seater. The extreme wraparound at the base of the gull-wing door allowed easy entry. A tubular frame was used, suggested in this view by the small frame rail by the seat. The interior looks very safe. Roger Stowers photo

Robin Hamilton with his first purpose-built racing V8s, which ended up with the Nimrods.

This car was built in 1975 at a sprint meeting! Roger Stowers photo

Robin Hamilton at Le Mans in 1967 in RHAM 1, his first Le Mans start and finish (seventeenth overall and third in class). Though some regarded the entry as a joke, Hamilton acquitted himself with honor. Aston enthusiasts who were present will not forget the emotions aroused by this race. Roger Stowers photo

Robin Hamilton returned to Le Mans in 1979 with this twin-turbine rebuild of RHAM 1 but retired after 2¾ hours. Roger Stowers photo

The Lola T70 Mark III GT, number SL73/103, with the 5064 cc Aston Martin V8 engine. This car was at Le Mans in 1967 and retired during the third lap. A second Lola-Aston was built, SL73/121. Roger Stowers photos

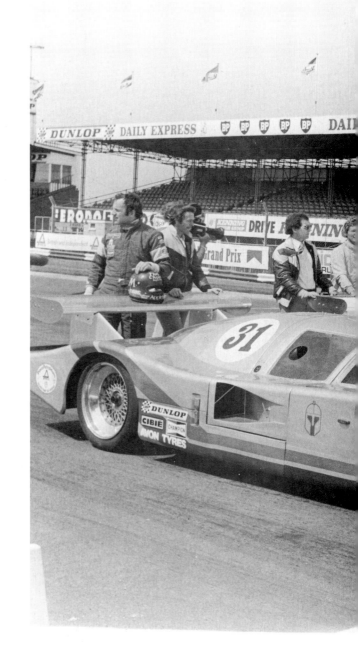

Press day for the first three Nimrods before the six-hour race in 1982. From left to right, numbers 1, 4 and 3. Roger Stowers photo

The first Nimrod next to DBR1/2. Left to right, James Hunt, Stirling Moss and, in the DBR, Roy Salvadori, Jack Fairman and (standing) Eric Thompson, all of whom were works drivers. Roger Stowers photo

John Downe entered this Nimrod at Le Mans in
1982, and it was doing very well until it crashed
after four hours. Roger Stowers photo

The Nimrods were developed and the works car
looked like this in 1984. Roger Stowers photo

The blinding speed of the Aston Martin V8s has attracted competition-minded enthusiasts.

This car was constructed by Ray Taft. Roger Stowers photo

A special built by David Ellis. The ingenuity in improving drag and the airfoil are evident.

Ellis has an impressive victory record. Roger Stowers photo

The Tojeiro-Aston, TAD/2/56, with engine VBJ/458, began competition in the late fifties and continues to race. It is nicer looking than its companion, TAD/4/56. Roger Stowers photo

Aston Martin engines, when installed in a Vauxhall Viva in this Pope Special, produce some blistering speeds but are a bit corner shy. Roger Stowers photo

Specifications

Year	Model	Engine size	Power/ rpm	Wheel- base	0-60 (Sec.)	Top speed	No. built
1923-25	touring	1486 cc sv	38/4000	8'9"	-		
1923-25	sports	1486 cc sv	45/4000	8'	-	72	
1923-25	super	1486 cc					
	Sports	16v-2 ohc	55/4200	8'	-	90	
						total	63
1927-29	T type	1495 cc ohc	56/4500	10'	-	70	
1929-32	International	1495 cc ohc	56/4500	8'6"	35	75	
	Ulster	1495 cc ohc	63/4750	9'10"		74	
						total	129
1932-33	New International	1495 cc ohc	60/4500	8'6"	23	70	
	Le Mans	1495 cc ohc	70/4750	8'6"	22	85	
	Std. 12/50	1495 cc ohc	55/4500	10'			
						total	130
1934-35	Mk II	1495 cc ohc	73/4700	8'6"	22	84	61
	Ulster	1495 cc ohc	80/5250	8'6"		95	21
	long saloon	1495 cc ohc	73/4750	10'	28	76	69+
1938-40	Speed model	1949 cc ohc	100/5000	8'3"	16	100	12
	15/98 short	1949 cc ohc	98/5000	8'3"	20	83	75
	15/98 long	1949 cc ohc	98/5000	9'8"			76
	C type	1949 cc ohc	110/5250	8'6"			8
1948-59	DB1	1970 cc ohv	90/4750	9'		85	

6-cylinder models

Year	Model	Engine size	Power/ rpm	Wheel- base	0-60 (Sec.)	Top speed	No. built
1950-53	DB2	2580 cc 2 ohc	105/5000, developed to 116/5000	8'3"	12	110	
	Vantage	2580 cc 2 ohc	125/5000	8'3"			
						total	411
1951-53	DB3	2580 cc 2 ohc	140/5300	7'9"			10
		2922 cc 2 ohc	163/5500				

Year	Model	Engine size	Power/rpm	Wheel-base	0-60 (Sec.)	Top speed	No. built
1953-55	DB2/4	2580 cc 2 ohc	125/5000	8'3"	12.6	111	
	(April 1954)	2922 cc 2 ohc	140/5000	8'3"	10.5	118	
						total	565
1953	DB3S	2922 cc 2 ohc	182/5000 (works)	7'3"			
1955	DB3S	2922 cc 2 ohc	240/6000 (works)	7'3"	6.6	140	11
	DB3S	2922 cc 2 ohc	180/5500 (production)	7'3"			19
1955-57	DB2/4 MkII	2922 cc 2 ohc	140/5000	8'3"	10	119	199
1957-59	DB MkIII	2922 cc 2 ohc	162/5500	8'3"	9	119	551
1956-60	DBR developed to plus several other engines to	2493 cc 2 ohc	212/7000	7'6"			
		2992 cc 2 ohc	258/7000				
		4164 cc	349/6000			197	
						total	14
1958-63	DB4	3670 cc 2 ohc	240/5500	8'2"	9	140	1110
1959-63	DB4GT	3670 cc 2 ohc	302/6000	7'9"	6	153	76
	Zagato	3670 cc 2 ohc	314/6000	7'9"			19
1963-65	DB5	3995 cc 2 ohc	282/5500	8'2"	8	145	
	Vantage	3995 cc 2 ohc	314/5750	8'2"			
						total	1021
1965-69	DB6	3995 cc 2 ohc	325/5750	8'6"	6.5	148	1504
1969-70	DB6 Mk2	3995 cc 2 ohc	325/5750	8'6"			278
1967-72	DBS	3995 cc 2 ohc	325/5750	8'7"	7	141	787
1972-73	AM Vantage	3995 cc 2 ohc	325/5750	8'7"			70

V8-engined models

Year	Model	Engine size	Power/rpm	Wheel-base	0-60 (Sec.)	Top speed	No. built
1970-72	DBSV8	5340 cc 4 ohc	375/6200	8'7"	6	160	399
1972-	AMV8	5340 cc 4 ohc	397/6200	8'7"	6	160	
						total	1900+
1977-	AMV8 Vantage	5340 cc 4 ohc	408/6200	8'7"	5.2	180	250+

The Aston Martin Owners Club (AMOC)

Membership in this distinguished 2,500 member club is essential for Aston Martin enthusiasts. Numerous publications are provided:

1. The *Aston Martin Magazine* is published quarterly and is of very high quality. It features many fine pictures, color covers and important articles.

2. The *Aston Martin News Sheet* appears monthly and contains news of events, and area and section news. A classified section is helpful for price information but the market represented is normally in the UK.

3. The *List of Members* is produced annually, an exceptionally valuable resource for new members seeking contacts and help.

4. The *Aston Martin Register* appears from time to time containing historical information on all models, competition histories of virtually all important cars, current ownership of cars in the club, and UK and Irish registration numbers.

The UK is divided into twenty areas, while overseas there are four major sections. In addition there are overseas representatives in various countries including six in Australia. Persons interested in joining the club may contact the following persons:

Paul Sabine
70 Glyndon Road
Camberwell 3124, Victoria, Australia

Jim Whyman, Secretary
Aston Martin Owners Club Ltd
Burtons Lane, Chalfont St Giles
Bucks, HP8 4BL England
(02404) 4742

Charles L. Turner
195 Mt. Paran Rd NW
Atlanta, GA 30327

Harvey Joliff
29873 Clearbrook Circle 146
Hayward, CA 94545

Tom O'Keefe
996 Bonnie Brae
Laguna Beach, CA 92651

Dr. Manfred Shlick
Oberer Reisberg 11, D-6830
Bad Homburg v.d. Hohe, West Germany

José M. Oliver
Dufourstrasse 65
CH-8702 Zollikon, Switzerland

Robert Follows
4125 Marine Drive
Vancouver VTV IN8 BC Canada

Nick Pryke
50 Lyndhurst Rd
Lyndhurst, Johannesburg 2192
So. Africa

Annotated bibliography

Bastow, Donald. *W. O. Bentley: Engineer.* Somerset, England:Haynes Publishing Group, 1978. 366 pages.

Often overlooked by Aston Martin enthusiasts, this book contains two chapters of special interest (chapters 11 and 13), which present important history of the 2.6 liter Lagonda engine. In particular, chapter 13 is a detailed technical description with numerous engineering calculations for out-of-balance shaft vectors, crankshaft inertias, bearing loads, spring stress analysis, big-end torque values and other items. This book will be useful to all owners of postwar models up to the DB4.

Bowler, Michael. *Automobile Quarterly*, vol. XXI, no. 4 (fourth quarter 1983):346ff.

Bowler has written a splendid, concise history of the firm which is followed by thirty-nine pages of beautiful color plates of most Aston Martin models. Bowler has had a fine racing career, is a well-known author, is the founding author of *Thoroughbred and Classic Cars*, and is the engineering director of the company.

_____. *Aston Martin V8*, Cadogan Publications Limited. 224 pages.

Bowler's association with the firm as engineering director and his broad experience in journalism and racing gives him a unique position to write with authority. This valuable book is essential reading for Aston Martin enthusiasts. A substantial history of the marque precedes the important material on the V8.

Candee, Richard A., comp. *Aston Martin in America*, ed. Halsey Bascom and Tony Krzczuk. Shaker Heights, Ohio:Vintage Motorpress, 1982. 500 copies.

This book is an effort in association with the American Aston Martin Owners Club East. It is a collection of helpful hints and maintenance instructions by members of the club on the post-1945 cars and is an important technical source, valuable for buyers searching out weaknesses in cars.

Coram, Dudley. *The Aston Martin Manual of Models 1921-1958.* London:Aston Martin Owners Club, 1965. 404 pages.

An excellent repair manual compiled with help from club members. Detailed specifications and substantial technical advice are included.

_____, comp. *The Aston Martin 1½ Litre International.* Middlesex, England:Horseless Carriage, 1973. 56 pages.

A spectacular color survey, in very large format, of one car, printed to a very high quality level in Japan. Reprint of the instruction book at the rear. Highly collectible, particularly for those interested in the prewar cars, especially the vintage Aston Martin.

_____, comp., with Inman Hunter and F. E. Ellis. *Aston Martin, The Story of a Sports Car.*

London:Motor Racing Publications, 1946. 343 pages plus substantial appendixes on racing results.

A classic and much sought after book, now out of print. The first serious history of the company and the cars.

Courtney, Geoff. *The Power Behind Aston Martin.* Oxford:Oxford Illustrated Press, 1978. Photography by Roger Stowers.

Fascinating interviews with Bertelli, Hill, Brown, Beach, Curtis, Woodgate and Norman provide primary source material for this book. Excellent and rare photographs are included.

Demaus, A. B. *Lionel Martin, A Biography.* Isleworth:Transport Bookman Publications, 1980.

Feather, Adrian M., comp. *The Aston Martin: A Collection of Contemporary Road Tests, 1921-1942.* Yorkshire:Scholarly Press, 1974. 80 pages.

A reprint of prewar road tests by British magazines covering models from the 1921 side-valve to the 1942 Atom.

_____, comp. *The Aston Martin, A Collection of Contemporary Road Tests, 1959-1969.* Yorkshire:Scholar Press, 1979. 144 pages.

A useful reprint of various tests in British and American motoring magazines. Covers models from the DB4 to the DBS Vantage.

Garnier, Peter, comp. *Aston Martin,* compiled from the archives of *Autocar* magazine. London:Hamlyn, 1982. 160 pages.

A fine, large-format collection of articles beginning in 1921. Useful for contemporary impressions. Good drawings and technical description. Sixteen pages of color plates.

Harvey, Chris. *Aston Martin and Lagonda.* Oxford:Oxford Illustrated Press, 1979. 244 pages.

A large-format book with twenty-six color plates covering the post-1945 period. It includes broad coverage of history and useful sections on strengths and weaknesses, what to look for, club history, personalities, road tests and competition history. A handsome book for the enthusiast.

Hunter, Inman. *Aston Martin 1914 to 1940: A Pictorial Review.* London:Transport Bookman Publications, 1976. 192 pages.

A fine, compact history of the prewar cars with many high-quality black-and-white illustrations and an appendix of technical illustrations. Hunter is a co-editor of the Aston Martin Register, and this book is the best single history of the prewar period.

McComb, F. Wilson. *Aston Martin V8s.* London:Osprey Publishing, 1981. 136 pages.

A compact, sharply written, informative volume essential for those buying the V8 models. Eight pages of color plates plus numerous black-and-white illustrations and specifications are provided.

Road & Track on Aston Martin, 1962-1984. Surrey, England:Brooklands Books, 1984. 88 pages.

A reprint collection of twenty-seven road tests and saloon studies, including one on a prewar model, one on a 1935 Ulster and five on the Lagonda. Identified authors include Tony Hogg, Cyril Posthumus, Doug Nye, Henry N. Manney III, John Lamm and Paul Frere. Good, sound research, driving impressions and fine writing.

Stowers, Roger. *Aston Martin Guide from 1948.* Middlesex, England:Transport Bookman Publications, 1979. 16 pages.

A brief model-by-model review with specifications and pictures, and a bibliography of road tests. Stowers has had a long and distinguished career with the company.

Whyte, Andrew. *The Aston Martin and Lagonda: Six-cylinder DB Models.* London:Motor Racing Publications, 1984. 144 pages.

A well-written history of the two marques with numerous appendixes dealing with introduction dates, specifications, chassis numbers, production records, engine identification, sports and racing cars and performance figures. In the Collector's Guide Series. Highly recommended for buyers of the David Brown models.